Every Youth Leader's
Emergency Guide Book

BOOK
SALE

Every Youth Leader's Emergency Guide Book

Neil O'Boyle

alpha

First published in 1999 by Alpha

05 04 03 02 01 00 99   7 6 5 4 3 2 1

Alpha is an imprint of Paternoster Publishing,
PO Box 300, Carlisle, Cumbria, CA3 0QS, UK
http://www.paternoster-publishing.com

British Library Cataloguing in Publication Data
A catalogue record for this book is available from the British Library

ISBN 1-898938-81-4

Cover design by Mainstream, Lancaster
Typeset by WestKey Limited, Falmouth, Cornwall
Printed in Great Britain by Caledonian International Book
Manufacturing Ltd, Glasgow

Dedication

I wish to dedicate this book to
D.
who asked for help when it was just too late.
You have inspired me to never reach that point again.

Contents

Foreword

Help!

Youth work is never tidy! Just when you think that you have solved one problem then Friday evening looms like a five-eyed creature from hell ready to devour your neat ideas about teenagers. But that is Friday and that's six days away. You console yourself that six days is six days. Then you listen to the answering machine telephone and you hear the bad news from Sue your co-worker who can't be there next week; she then announces that she has heard that Jane the new fourteen-year-old blonde bombshell is wildly in love with you. Your fiancee has just heard this phone call and she is angrily demanding why you led her on!! You remonstrate that you just smiled and . . . . . .!

This book provides some clear and direct answers in a way that does not treat you like last year's Christmas tree. It tackles real issues in a lively manner and faces the tough issues youth leaders face without making you think that you're a moron.

Neil is a face to face youth worker and has been there and seen most of the highs and lows of youth ministry. He has a positive attitude and the clear and helpful stories, advice and direction given is derived from the years of youth ministry in London. He is practical and gives you byte-size information in a format which provides the FIRST AID which most of us require on a regular basis.

I commend this book to you. There is nothing else like it. Neil serves youth by serving you. Use it . . . Friday night is coming!!

Thank you

Bob Moffett

Bob and his wife Jilly have been in youth ministry for the last 23 years. Bob until recently was on the World Leadership of Youth For Christ International

Acknowledgements

I wish to express my deepest gratitude to the following people or groups:

Dr Ian Milne – my father-in-law who has spent many hours checking, questioning and affirming every word I have written. Thanks Ian!

Patrick Bateman and Dr Ruth Marchant for giving their wisdom and insight on the more sensitive subjects.

British Youth for Christ – who have provided valuable information for me throughout the book and who took a great risk by giving me Greenwich as a young and inexperienced youth worker.

Alison Hull who worked both hard and creatively as my Copy Editor for Paternoster.

St. John's Church, Blackheath, for your continual support and encouragement and to Searchlight and Legacy, for adopting me not only as your youth pastor for four and a half years, but also as your friend. I have learned so much from you guys!

Paul and Sheelagh Easby, Phil Collins and my dear friend Theo – my mentors.

Joy, my wife and most faithful friend, who has stood by me from the very beginning.

How to use this book

'Every Youth Leader's Emergency Guide-Book' is aimed at helping those youth leaders who, like myself, find themselves continually in trouble, for one reason or another! Its style and content are modelled on a First Aid book. When you twist your ankle or get stung by a wasp, the correct treatment is not always obvious, and it is helpful to have a simple medical guide at your fingertips. This book has twenty-six chapters offering help when you are in trouble or when something has actually gone wrong in your ministry. It also lays down some healthy guidelines.

I have yet to meet the youth leader, voluntary or waged, full- or part-time, who hasn't at one time or other got out of their depth. Each chapter highlights an issue with which I (or someone I have worked with) have struggled. In many cases, we failed and ended up as casualties (occasionally literally!) The book is born out of the recognition, during such incidents, of the need for immediate practical help.*

The book can be approached in two ways. It can be read straight through in an evening, or it can be used as reference as the problem arises. It offers first-aid, reassurance and guidelines for good practice. Each chapter has the format of a medical text, as follows

Problem: The subject is identified (e.g. when is sex right?).

---

* The practical help suggested in this book can only be of a general nature and may not fit into more complex, complicated or very different circumstances to the ones mentioned.

Category: The subject is classified. (e.g. young people, sex and relationships).

Symptoms: Illustrations (perhaps a little exaggerated) to help you relate to the subject.

Case history: A true story that brings the problem under discussion to life.**

Care plans: This is the 'meat' of the chapter where you can find the answers and ways of dealing with the problem.

Action page: 21 chapters have either an activity, illustration or guidelines for you to refer to for further help.

The final chapter lists further resources – suggestions for further reading or organisations that can help.

I've always wanted to be the best youth worker possible for God, the young people I work with and my employer and I'm sure you have a similar desire. However, reality has taught me that although just loving and being able to relate to young people are essential, more than these two basic qualities are required to be a safe and effective youth worker. I hope that this book will help you with all the issues that you are grappling with, and also that it will help you to avoid some of the painful mistakes others have made.

** In order to maintain the integrity and protection of the people mentioned in various stories I have changed both names and environments when appropriate.

PROBLEM
How can I have a successful youth programme?

Category   *A creative youth programme that works*

Symptoms   *Playing 'Demolish the youth worker's house' seems to be more attractive than your Bible teaching, and is bringing in new members each week. You're struggling each week to come up with something that will hold their attention.*

Case History

'Jenny!' called Mrs Bailey to her daughter who had one foot out of the door. 'Are you going to church again?' Jenny placed both her feet back in the house. 'I thought you liked me going to church', Jenny replied, more as a statement than a question. 'I do, but this is the third time this week. What's going on? I used to have to drag you there on Sundays'. Mrs Bailey was clearly puzzled by the change of heart in her daughter. 'Well, this new youth worker has really changed things, he makes things fun. I mean, it's still serious but it's enjoyable as well'. Mrs Bailey raised her eyebrows, and Jenny took that as permission to leave. 'Praise God!' Mrs Bailey exclaimed under her breath, heading for the telephone to let 'that' new youth worker know he was doing something right.

Care plans

In a culture where change occurs frequently, young people are losing the ability to concentrate for long periods of time. They quickly grow bored, distracted by other things or the people around them. The days when leaders stood in front of a group, teaching intently for an extended period of time, are increasingly a thing of the past.

Having toured recently with Bob Moffett (formerly on the world leadership team for Youth For Christ International), I have never failed to be impressed with his desire, when training leaders, to communicate that youth workers must show Christianity is fun. For what good is it to say 'Christ offers life', while we look as miserable as sin? The same principle should be applied to our programmes. We want every programme we hold to be packed to the doors with young people, but in reality this is seldom the case. However, if the youth group is fun, enjoyable and attractive, then over a period of time, we will experience growth.

There is a statistic that says if we simply lecture young people then, three hours later, they will remember seventy per cent of what we said. Three days later they will only remember ten per cent. We want to be more effective than this! Not only do we want young people to enjoy what we do for them, we want them to remember what has been taught.

Good communicators don't just try to grip their audience by word but are visual, with plenty of illustrations. Now if we combine the VISUAL with the VERBAL, young people remember eighty-five per cent of what they heard and saw three hours later. Three days later, it has been reduced to sixty-five per cent. Most of us, if we are honest, would be pleased if members of our group could remember sixty-five per cent of what we said three days later.

Yet there is an even more effective way of learning. When people are involved in DOING (kinetic learning as opposed to static), their thought processes and imagination are stimulated to get to grips with problematic issues. As a result they remember an estimated ninety-five per cent three hours later and some eighty-five per cent three days later. Wow!! Learning by doing (kinetic), in group or individual teaching, is head and shoulders above all other forms of remembering.

We desire excellence, so we must create the most enjoyable learning environment, with plenty of variety. In our programmes we should seek to combine constant change with the three styles of learning: hearing, seeing and doing. There isn't a statistic for how much is remembered when all three are operating together, but it is going to be higher than eighty-five per cent three days later.

If, five minutes into the meeting, your group have that glazed look over their eyes, and facial expressions that say they wish they were somewhere else, with constant glances at their wrist watches, I would suggest you do an entire evaluation of your programme.

As soon as Jesus showed up, crowds flocked to hear him speak, captivated by what he said. His communicative creativity was flawless. He drew people from afar to hear him, using illustrations and stories to fire their imaginations and to stimulate thought.

To produce these electric and creative programmes, we as youth workers must use our own imaginations. Being fun and stimulating, week in, week out on grey days, rainy days, black days and red hot sunny days is no easy task. However there are plenty of books to help us in this area.

Action Page

The Classic Youth Meeting

This is the framework that I have adopted and many other youth workers have used over the years. Four framework principles for any programme:

- Breaker

  Usually an active, full moving, crazy ice-breaker that involves everybody and leads into illustrating the topic of the meeting. Give at least ten minutes to it, allowing the group to relax and feel at ease with one another and their environment. If time allows, the more games the better.

- Entertainment

  This is the part where the group teaching begins, but rather than launch into a long spoken explanation, it is made far more visual and interactive than verbal. For example, if the evening meeting was on 'Value' then, with a water pistol, take a member of the group hostage (you need to play the part of a real-life kidnapper). Blindfold them, strap them to a chair, put the pistol to their head and ask the group to ransom them. The person who pays the highest price in sweets or hard currency (make sure it doesn't get too silly, and remember to give the payment to the hostage afterwards), gets the hostage as a slave for the rest of the meeting, to make him or her a drink/ get them biscuits etc. Choose someone willing and who likes a laugh. Go on to talk about the value of human life . . . The aim of the entertainment is to be visual and fun and to set the scene for the evening.

- Stimulation

  This is the heart of the meeting, by far the most important part, for it is here that maximum learning takes place. At least half of the meeting should be dedicated to this. Those of you like me, who just love to speak, should exercise discipline here. Stimulation can be done in a whole variety of ways, from interactive group exercises to more contemplative individual approaches. Here are some examples:

- Group discussion, Bible studies, task activities, debates, buzz groups, working groups, work sheets, questionnaires and imagination activities. Make sure they are packed with activity, whether motion, interactive or reflective. Just stimulate and then allow the young people to discover and work through issues with their peers or on their own. Thinking leads to discovery, discovery leads to learning and remembering.
- Challenge

  Conclude the meeting by rounding up the points that have come from stimulation as well as going on to give clear precise biblical teaching with a challenge and encouragement (using if possible visual and verbal illustrations) for the young people to take with them.

To this framework I would add worship, and prayer. I would also add anything remotely wacky (controlled fun) to keep the meeting alive! The style can be used on eleven-year-olds, fifteen-year-olds and eighteen-year-olds. The content would change dramatically for each age group, but the framework is still appropriate.

In another chapter I have implied that young people do not grow with just fun and games alone, and I still maintain this is true. Clear biblical truths wrapped in the three principles of learning: hearing, seeing and doing, combined with the four point framework of creative programmes: breaker, entertainment, stimulation and challenge will bring about plenty of learning, interaction, fun and growth! God's word and the Christian path are both very serious and life changing. We shouldn't compromise these in order to be trendy. Nor should we compromise spiritual growth and learning by wanting to appear too serious. Learning can be and should be fun. As youth leaders we must be committed to portraying Christianity as fun, enjoyable and life giving. If that's the case, our programmes will be a place where young people want to be.

PROBLEM
How important are numbers?

Category   *The importance of size*

Symptoms   *Trying to lead a group discussion with just one young person.*
120 people in the living room means a crushed frenzy rather than a Bible Study.
Can I have a popular youth group without compromising on the spiritual bits.

Case History

Taking on a new role as youth Pastor for an Anglican church in south-east London, I had inherited a youth group of some forty young people and four leaders. For the first three months or so, I was fairly excited about the group and where things were going.

However, as time progressed, I shared with the leaders about my growing concern that the group were not receiving any real spiritual teaching. It wasn't through lack of trying – all the leaders had done their utmost to teach and challenge the teenagers but whenever they did so, the group reacted in a hostile manner. They seemed only to want fun, games and social outings. They would tolerate some input but only as long as it wasn't 'heavy'. After a great deal of thought and consultation with the other leaders, I decided it was no longer going to be a youth fellowship group which neither heard the gospel, nor about living out the values we claimed to believe. From then on, week in and week out, we passionately taught the gospel and Christian values. Over a period of four months the group deteriorated from forty young people to less than ten.

Needless to say I received my fair share of criticism, but the leaders and I had made the decision and we stuck with it. The ten or so young people who remained over the following year grew in their faith in ways they had never grown before. They now had a real live faith, understood salvation and had an unquestionable love for Jesus. We continued in our decision to teach a real gospel without compromise and over the following three years the youth work in the church grew to over forty fired-up young people.

Care Plans

Most of us, if we are honest, would like our youth groups to be numerically on the larger size. For the majority of leaders the reality is the opposite. Most of us experience groups of ten to fifteen young people. Many leaders in more rural settings (where young people are not overflowing) have groups as low as four or five teenagers. Those leaders with groups between twenty-five to forty youngsters are viewed with great admiration and envy. Those few exceptions who have weekly youth fellowship groups as large as one hundred or more are viewed as super youth leaders who are in a highly elite and successful league of their own.

After each Bible study or weekly youth meeting, many of us sink into the back of a chair with a mug of coffee, wondering how we will ever build up the size of our meetings. What does it take to attract new members, what are we doing so badly wrong and what new trendy style do we need to adopt to be the coolest and most relevant church youth group in the area?

We may well have the best possible motives for wanting a larger group but more often than not numbers are a false security and can be a bar to what we wish to achieve. If we take Jesus as our example, we would have to note he had no problems with numbers. Crowds followed him wherever he went and daily he rose to teach them. Yet the reality is Jesus was always keen to be away from the masses; he was much more concerned to be around the few disciples whom he had hand picked. It was with the few rather than the many that he poured out all his wisdom and knowledge. Many of us, if given a choice, would rather preach to the crowds than talk and teach a handful of believers, but it was this handful that went on to change the world.

So we shouldn't despair if our Sunday youth fellowship group is unable to fill the Royal Albert Hall. The basic thing we need to stick to is that we want quality above and beyond quantity, and if we have quality success breeds success. In my own situation, only when I had lost those who did not share my direction and had created a small nucleus of young people who enjoyed being in the meetings, did I see fruit in their individual lives and fruit in the growth of the group.

The simple fact of the matter is far more will be achieved in a youth group of eight members where one leader can comfortably pour everything he or she knows into the lives of that small group than can ever be achieved in a group of fifty young people.

Naturally we all want youth meetings of fifty or more young people but if we expect maximum growth then the fifty should be divided into five smaller groups. If you have a large youth group, by all means start your meetings together for games, worship, announcements, general gossip and any introductory teaching, but if you stay together for a long period of teaching, sharing and discussion minimum growth will be achieved. It's far better to split into smaller groups for the bulk of the time and become one group again at the end.

From my experience of leading large groups of young people all packed into a living room, I can say that issues such as control, attention and distraction become a real problem. The core principles of learning such as listening, seeing, doing and sharing are not easy to achieve. The group dynamics of ten to twelve people are very different from the dynamics of a group of fifty young people. Small core groups should be developed where young people can express themselves freely. It is in such an environment, rather than in a crammed room, listening to a leader speak for a long period of time with little or no interaction, that growth will occur.

A successful group is where numbers are less important than the individual and where an environment is created for growth. All good things start small!

Action Page

 • How big is your youth group?

• Over the last year has it grown/declined/ remained the same?

• What is the ideal size you want for your group?

• In what ways do you put quality above quantity?

• Do you ever put quantity above quality? If so, how?

• Are you seeing numerical growth?

• If you are not seeing growth what course of action do you have in mind (if any)?

• How are you balancing the importance for individual spiritual growth alongside numerical growth?

PROBLEM
How do I know when things are going off the rails?

Category   *Evaluation*

Symptoms   *You notice members of the group have brought copies of 'Loaded' and 'Computer Shopper' to the Bible study.*
At the end of the meeting one of the young people makes the comment 'Youth group would be perfect if we just dropped the religious stuff altogether!'

Case History

The Saturday night group was experiencing growth. It had previously consisted of twelve girls and two boys. Over the last year Brian and the other leaders had prayed for more males to join the group. All of a sudden eight males arrived over the course of a month. The next month saw two more join. None of the new arrivals were believers, but Brian had plans about that.

But as time went by, Brian became concerned with the lack of overall spiritual growth. The direction of the group had changed, mainly in order to cater for the needs of the new members. This meant the believing members were no longer receiving quality teaching. After four months or so the group had gone from a strong emphasis on biblical teaching to a real mess. At some meetings the Bible wasn't even brought out and it became rare for God to be mentioned for more than five minutes in any week. The new members just seemed so disinterested in anything to do with God, that Brian was caused finally to wonder why they had joined in the first place. The answer hit him like a brick: his group had twelve unusually attractive girls who all seemed beyond their years in physical appearance. Brian now realised that God was the last thing on these new boys' minds. The Saturday night fellowship had turned from a Bible study into a glorified social club.

Care Plans

As all hell is breaking loose around you in the middle of a youth meeting, has the thought: 'Why do I bother to come?' ever occurred to you? Nobody seems to be interested in anything other than talking about the latest TV programme, who the fittest girl in the room is or what slanderous juicy gossip is available. The leader at the front is having as much influence as a zebra in front of a lion and the poor worship leader has gone home in tears at the simple fact nobody bothered to sing – they didn't even notice someone was playing the guitar. The only thing that stopped them between idle chit-chat was to ask what had happened to the coffee and biscuits.

Youth groups can be more like trips to the zoo or circus some weeks and at the end of the meeting you feel like you have gone twelve rounds with a heavyweight boxer. You slump back into the chair and think silently: 'Why do I do this?' The answer is you do it because you are a hero! However, it is better to be a live healthy hero than a dry exhausted dying hero.

If you find yourself asking 'Why do I do this' then the chances are you need to be asking some more questions such as

- What is the purpose of the youth work?
- Why was it ever set up in the first place?
- What are we achieving?

Over time, youth work can either enter a rut or else take a quite different path than you ever intended. For a successful ministry we need to frequently and brutally evaluate what we are doing; the original purpose and the reality of what we are achieving. I have many times found myself drifting around like a lost dinghy in the sea, with a vague idea of where I should be going but with the vastness of the work drowning any sense of direction. It's easy to sit back and just continue bobbing along; it actually takes brave leaders to put the anchor down and start looking at what went wrong and how we can get out of the mess we are in.

Stage 1 What are we actually doing?
With other leaders take a pen and sheet of paper and write down what you are doing in your youth meetings (not what you want to do or intended to do). For example *Sunday fellowship group – twenty people – Bible study on life styles – Some worship and some prayer*.

Stage 2 Is it working?
Now with honesty and guts admit whether what you are doing is worth the effort or a waste of time. *E.g. Sunday fellowship group – Bible study – teaching is OK though never any feedback, group work discussion always goes off track, worship is dreadful and prayer is nothing other than silence.*

Stage 3 What was the original aim?
Are you doing what you set out to do, or have you gone in a different direction altogether? If you have taken a different route, is it one which you are happy with?

E.g. *Sunday Fellowship group – was set up for positive Bible study, most of which was supposed to be group work and discussion. Now it is nearly all up-front teaching.*

Stage 4 Do you need to change the aims?
Now that you have considered what you are doing, whether it is working and whether it is what you set out to do, ask yourself; 'Has the time come to make changes or am I happy with the course of action taken?' For some this may mean minor changes while for others it may require a complete overhaul.

At times what you have achieved is exactly what you set out to do, but as you reflect you realise it still doesn't work. This can be incredibly distressing and disappointing. Before you point the finger at yourself for being a poor visionary and a hopeless achiever, ask the following questions:

Did I plan the programme for the number of young people who actually attend?
Adventurous programmes with either too many or too few young people can end up falling flat. Fifty people sharing something about themselves one at a time could go on far longer than expected as well as problems of disruption. Five people splitting into three working groups may prove impossible!

Did I estimate the level of spiritual or emotional maturity of the group when planning the programme?
Content that is too shallow, deep, heavy or light can frustrate and even insult members of your group. Eighteen-year-olds may not want to play twelve-year-old icebreaker games, while twelve-year-olds may not be able to sit through a sixty-minute debate on sanctification. Even committed mature believers may struggle meeting all the time with unbelievers who are either merely looking or just not interested.

Did I plan the programme with the right venue in mind?
This is a simple but vital issue which is easy to get wrong. Is this venue right for the particular programme I have planned, and for these particular young people? Games need open space, while verbal teaching works better in a closed space. Large groups need room; group work needs several rooms. People need to be warm or cool depending on the weather. Hard floors need chairs or cushions but the room mustn't be so cluttered that I can't see what is happening. The venue can ruin our programmes if it doesn't fit the needs of the group and what we have planned.

Did my plan take into account the quality of leaders I had?
Leaders can make or kill programmes. A bad leader is like a migraine: hard to treat! Having to be at the centre of attention at all times, he talks and giggles through another leader's message. He disrupts the prayer time by playing footsie with a bunch of teens, and thinks male bonding is attacking every boy in the group, dragging them onto the floor and twisting their limbs until they beg for mercy . . . A good leader is a Godsend. Fully

supportive and encouraging, they have only one agenda, to help and be helpful. With a natural ability to find an area of need, they promptly fill it. How helpful are the leaders you work with at helping you to achieve your goals?

Did my plan take into account the quantity of leaders I had?
In addition to how good or bad the leaders are, is the programme too ambitious for the human resources you have available? Did you brief them in advance or did the programme frequently stop for dialogue and explanation?

Was the timing of the programme suitable?
The best programmes in the world fail because of timing. Is it too early or too late, is Saturday or Sunday the best night for it? Are members of your group committed to other things that conflict? Make sure any programme is entirely practical for the physical and social needs of your group.

Action Page

Paul urges his readers in 1Corinthians 14:40: 'Everything should be done in a fitting and orderly way'.

Take another blank piece of paper, and hold all the evaluation notes not too far from you as you begin to think through the next question. If we started everything again, what would we do? Before you can answer that question you need to be sure you can answer these next questions:

* What is your overall vision?
* What are your aims for achieving that vision for the next term, one year, three years, five years?
* Who are you aiming at?
* What are their physical, social, emotional, mental and spiritual needs?
* When, where and for how long will you meet?
* Who are your leaders?

With these questions and your previous experience, you are in a good position to plan afresh. In a month's time, you may sit in a meeting and realise you haven't asked that familiar question 'What am I doing here?' Going off the tracks and having directionless youth groups is all too common. With good evaluation and subsequent action, your changes will make the difference between a struggling, stationary ministry and a slick and successful youth group with purpose and direction.

COMPLAINT
Not the youth weekend again?

Category *Surviving nights away*

Symptoms *Bloodshot eyes and nightly panic attacks leading up to the event.*
Fear of losing another kid over a cliff.

Case History

The Christian Summer Vacation Trust had just employed a new camp director for the coming summer. There would be 120 young people attending this year's six week camp, which was set in acres of redwood trees. The forest had proved a successful camp site for years. Jim, the camp director, had worked hard at getting everything ready. The day came and buses arrived, full of tired but excited teenagers, who rolled out and started to choose their bunks in the cabins.

The first couple of days went by and Jim hadn't been spotted by anyone apart from first thing on a morning and last thing at night. A week went by and it was still the same – he was nowhere to be seen. Many great things had begun to happen with the young people and conversions were a daily occurrence. Some of the kids who had been sick or had disfigurements had miraculously been healed. There was a touch of God at this camp that had not been present at any other throughout the years. After nearly two weeks, the board of trustees visited the site and heard that Jim had not been around. He was summoned and made to account for himself. He reluctantly told the trustees that he spent twelve hours of the day – every day – in prayer. Somewhat taken aback by his response, they replied 'But Jim, you're the co-ordinator. We employed you to mix with the kids, relate to them, bring them to faith, and teach them God's word. Not to pray!' Jim explained there were other gifted leaders who could do that but he believed his time was best spent in prayer. 'What about meal times?' a trustee asked 'You don't even show up then?' 'No'. Jim responded 'I'm fasting for the first four weeks'. His reply was not well received. After a moment of murmuring, the chair of the trustees informed Jim his services were no longer required at the camp. He had missed the point of why he should be there and was dismissed.

Care Plans

A paradox of a story. The trustees want a relational co-ordinator for the six weeks, someone who can relate well to the kids, but the co-ordinator wants to spend that time in more constructive ways. Without question his prayers were seeing results. Things were happening in new and fresh ways. Yet he wasn't doing what he was paid to do. What would you do if you were the chair of the trustees?

It's not easy to measure things of spiritual value, in contrast with the more easily recognisable hands-on youth work, but it is likely the trustees lost the best worker they have ever had.

For many leaders, youth camps and residential trips are the highlight of the year, yet they are the biggest headache to organise. But we invest much time, money and effort into going away with the group because weekends away, house parties, camps and retreats are all great for reaching the core goals of youth work. These are

- Deepening a young person's relationship with God
- Deepening the young person's relationships with other members of the group
- Deepening the young person's relationships with the leaders

You may have other agendas too, but these goals are paramount. Needless to say in achieving them an abundance of fun should be included. The most successful weekends away are the ones that are best organised. Don't run your camp on an ad-lib basis; it doesn't usually work. Be fully prepared. Make sure you have

- Booked the site and paid any deposits.
- Organised safe transport with driver (if required).
- Your cooks, kitchen utensils and meal plans in order.
- Collected your food and full list of equipment (e.g. toilet paper).
- A full programme plan which leaves no minute unaccounted for. There may well be free time but it should be written into the programme.
- Reserved the event beforehand for any external activities: e.g. horse riding, ice rink, swimming pool, canoes etc . . . Ensure qualified staff, e.g., a life guard, is available for appropriate activities.
- A full list of attendants with completed guardian forms (if required).
- Left a list of names and parent contacts with someone who is not attending the camp, whom both you and the parents can contact. and who can contact you.
- Information on all allergies and health problems. Do not take on camp anyone who poses a serious risk.
- A first-aider and adequate first aid equipment. Find out where the nearest hospital is and the telephone number of a local doctor whom you may contact if necessary.

It doesn't follow that the best camps are the most expensive. On the contrary, the best weekends away that I've been involved with have been low budget, sleeping in scruffy accommodation with no heating in the middle of nowhere. With your programmes, use the environment to the best of its potential e.g. mountains for walks, forests make great wide games, rivers for swimming – but make sure it is safe to do so.

So what do you fill your programme with? Here are five suggestions to make your camp experience complete

- **Eating:** More eating and even more eating: inside, outside, barbecues: just fill their faces.

- **Wild game slots:** These don't have to be 'pull-the-building-down-wild', just 'exhaust-them-wild'. Wild games, night games, assault courses, storm the building: make it worth remembering. Make it messy, with lots of mud, lots of food in your face, lots of madness.
- **External activities:** Hiking, night walks, go-kart racing: make sure they want to do them.
- **Worship and teaching:** Good worship and great speakers can make these life-time experiences. Bad worship and boring speakers can make it as dull as a graveyard.
- **Free time:** Let them spend time recovering from all of the above. Not too much but enough for them to have their space and do their thing. This can be a great time for leader relationships.

Use every moment to your advantage. Make them work, for example preparing food, washing up (these can be great times. Granted, you may have to chase after them, but it's still fun.) Bed time is where every leader's gifting is tested; allow noise, expect it to calm down then demand quietness. They may physically survive the camp but when school on Monday comes and they are too tired to go, their parents won't come visiting with gifts.

When you are planning for your camp, don't forget the story of Jim. Let's be relational and let's have as much fun with the young people as we can, but take time out before the camp, during the camp and after the camp to pray and ask God to move in a new and special way.

So be creative, fresh and different: be highly organised and have a great time.

Action Page

The following adapted recommendations are based upon Youth for Christ guidelines to respecting the individual and legal requirements for residential work with children under the age of eighteen. They are not intended to restrict but to safeguard all concerned from the potential of abuse.

- In residential work, do not invade the privacy of young people unnecessarily. Leaders should knock before entering dormitory accommodation and, except for emergencies, should only enter the accommodation of young people of the same sex.
- Separate accommodation for the sexes and also for the leaders, if possible: if not, then the leaders to sleep with their same sex group.
- Same age groups should be kept together in dormitories/rooms/tent.
- Leaders must be of the same sex as the young people attending. Mixed groups demand both sex leaders.
- For residential work longer than ninety days, or where a young person under the age of eighteen is employed by the organisation and living away from home, the organisation or church shall register both with their local Social Services department and the location's Social Services department when using a specific venue.
- Where mini bus drivers are used it is expected that all drivers and leaders will adhere to the legal and local authority regulations, when appropriate.
- A public telephone that is in working order must be within reachable distance. Mobile phones should not be considered public.

Thanks to Phil Collins, National Evangelist with YfC, for the illustration.

PROBLEM
Why don't members of my group change and resemble Christians?

Category   *Youth discipleship*

Symptoms   *As soon as church finishes, the youth group sneak behind a pew, get the cans out and discuss late night TV.*
When it comes to Bible study or watching 18-rated movies, the movie wins every time.
The youth group has moved away from church and now meets at the local pub.

Case History

The fellowship group had been a great success that particular week, with a lively discussion all about honesty and godly living. Tony, the leader, came away encouraged with the response of the group, feeling they had really begun to develop. The church weekend away was in a week's time and Tony had received pressure from numerous parents asking if he could try and persuade many of the youth to attend it. In reality, very few of the young people wanted to go, seeing it as boring and irrelevant. What neither Tony nor the parents had realised was that many of the young people had alternative plans, while their parents were away. Over the weekend, one house became the central meeting place for most of the youth group. On the Saturday night, dozens of bottles and cans of alcohol were smuggled into the house and the group drank to their hearts' content. While somewhat under the influence, they recklessly headed for the local night clubs.

It wasn't until after 2 a.m. that the bunch of fifteen or so early-to mid-teens finally returned to the house where they drank some more and then males and females crashed on the floor for what was later described as a harmless night's sleep. Apart from bad heads and frequent chucking down the toilet, the group thought they had got away with it, but to their dismay many people had seen and heard them over the course of the night and it wasn't long before parents were notified. Tony was the most affected by the incident. He felt he had failed, both in his teaching and in his role as youth worker. He had let himself be deceived by the appearance of the group who had spoken so eloquently and wisely the week before on honesty and godliness!

Care plans

There is something particularly disappointing and discouraging for a youth leader who has been responsible for the spiritual development of a youth group for several years, to discover one or more members have in one way or other deceived you. Finding out that someone smokes, takes drugs, drinks like a fish, is involved in theft, fights or sleeps around, can wound leaders as it wounds their parents. You feel a failure. You thought you understood the individual, you knew where they were at. They seemed to answer correctly to questions in the group, seemed to worship and pray in a style you would expect from a mature Christian. You believed they were open and honest, while secretly they were doing things many would not expect of a believer.

And yet if we were asked to place hand on heart and say, of some of the worst offenders in our groups, whether we believe them to be Christians or not, we may well respond that we believe they are. It is not safe to say 'well, he secretly smokes' or 'she periodically gets drunk' and then write them off as unbelievers. However, one can't help scratching one's head and saying: 'What has happened to the dying of their old nature, and where is the fruit of their faith?'

We must be committed to raising godly young people who are set apart for Jesus. We should set our aims, for each one of the teenagers in our care, that they become 'mature, attaining to the whole measure of the fullness of Christ' (Eph. 4:13). We should push and teach that Christ be the Lord of every area of their lives; their desires, their possessions, social lives, home lives and habits. There should not be an area that has not been submitted to his Lordship and control.

Yet there is an issue here of being real and facing up to the reality of adolescence and personal growth. If we just take ourselves (non-adolescents), think for a moment back to last time we actually sinned. If you are like me you probably don't have to go too far back. Of course your salvation, faith, belief and general self-discipline are not in question. You may not have committed such blatant examples of wrongful behaviour as your teenager, but your position as a more mature Christian means that your sin is just as great a sin as theirs, if not greater. If you, as a mature believer, fail, then what can we expect of those who do not have the same level of maturity or years of Christian service?

Try for a moment to step back into your own shoes as a fifteen-year-old. At that age I wasn't a believer and I felt free to indulge in as much pleasure as I wanted. Yet we may place unfair expectations upon Christian fifteen-year-olds, believing, in a kind of mythical way, that because they are Christians they will not struggle over the pleasures their peers freely indulge in.

How many fellowship groups or Bible studies have we attended where we have agreed what is right and what is sinful and yet we go away and continue to do the same sins? We know what is right: we want to walk the right path, but still now and again we fail. Paul says 'For the things I want to do I do not do, and the things I don't want to do I do.' (Rom. 7:15). Young people are the same – they know what is right and perhaps, 90 per cent of the time, they achieve it but for some 10 per cent they fail. It is true that when young people fool around and get involved in sin, they usually do it in a way seen by the whole Christian community. But it's also true that when mature believers sin it rarely leaves their own four walls. We are just more subtle! In addition, we need to remember the words of Jesus when he challenged the teachers of the law and the Pharisees 'He that is without sin can cast the first stone' (Jn. 8:7).

We should not condone the wrong actions of members of our group, any more than we condone the sin in our own lives. It is important to point out, again and again, right from wrong and why something is right or wrong. The issues of holiness, and how God has called us to walk a narrow path that is set apart from others, are essential to the development of our teenagers. Teaching on how Jesus does not call us to walk alone, but has given us himself and his Spirit as a source of strength and support, should be repeated at every opportunity. Equally we should sympathise with them when they recognise the way of the gospel can be hard. We must encourage young people in the areas where they are exhibiting discipline and strength, and where we can see them bearing fruit in their lives, as well as in those areas where they are struggling. When a young individual in our group is discovered doing something wrong, or has bravely confessed, of course we are disappointed. It is tempting to heap guilt beyond measure upon them so they may learn, but I don't think a 'guilt trip' is necessarily the answer. The gospel is one of forgiveness and grace. Therefore, with a full understanding of what they have done, we should seek out their real repentance, supported by the knowledge of the full cleansing of sin that Jesus offers (1 Jn. 1:7). In other words 'You have said you're sorry, Jesus forgives you, so let's forget it!'

What can we do to help reduce future failures? We must actively teach young people to hate sin. For if people do not hate the sin they have been snared by, then they are unlikely to see the error of their ways, and in the long term hardly likely to change. There will be no motive to do so. But if they come to hate the sin, then they will desire change and in the long term they will see fruit in their lives again.

The responsibility lies with you, as the youth leader who carries the burden for the group's spiritual growth, to see them develop in faith and manifest the fruit of the Spirit (Gal. 5:22–25). We should teach biblical truths, make time for one-to-one relationships so we truly understand the issues involved in individual's lives. Give guidance and counsel, be supportive and encouraging. Most of all be real with young people, expect mistakes, expect big blunders!

Try not to make it personal – it's hardly your fault. Be committed to them in prayer for in reality, changed hearts and minds only come about through the operation of the Spirit. When they do fail, don't leave them in the hole but give them a hand to get out again. Paul, in Philippians 3:12, clearly points out he has not yet achieved perfection but he continues in pursuit of this goal. If we persevere with those hardened offenders, they also will persevere in their faith! In time the fruit of the words you have sown in their hearts will begin to germinate, and signs of growth and maturity will emerge in their lives.

Action Page

- Don't set impossible goals.
- Expect failure.
- Be there for them.
- Continue to disciple them.
- Stick to teaching absolutes.
- Allow the Spirit to breathe life and direction into their lives.
- Believe this will lead them to reach maturity.

PROBLEM
Is faith inherited or chosen?

Category   *Churched young people syndrome*

Symptoms   *Five of your longest and most faithful young believers have decided to give up their faith and then come back to God in one month's time, so they can experience conversion.*
The youth group have requested that the drug Ecstasy be handed out in meetings as nothing seems fresh or exciting anymore.

Case History

John was leading this particular week in front of a group of eighteen young people. He was in his mid-twenties, incredibly eloquent, always holding everyone's attention. Today he was challenging everyone to seize hold of the life that Jesus offered, to the full. 'Don't take hold of the edges of God's good things and don't cling to life's dregs!' The entire group were almost out of their seats listening intently to every word. Towards the end of the meeting, Louise, started shuffling in her seat. John noticed and asked if she was OK.

'Not really' she replied. 'I've gone to church ever since I can remember and my parents have talked to me about things to do with God all my life. I read my Bible every night, I pray for thirty minutes a day. But I don't have life to the full. I feel void and empty. . . . it just doesn't seem to work. Perhaps God doesn't feel I'm worth the effort'.

Care Plans

In most youth fellowship groups, there are young people who have always been involved in the church, raised as Christians by God-fearing parents, who have encouraged their children to attend church ever since they can remember. Such young people come with the correct answer to every question you raise in youth fellowship; they know almost everything you will say before you say it. Confident praying aloud, they are usually actively evangelising within their own school. They are very precious and special to have as a part of your group, for they hold a rich foundation of biblical truths and moral standards.

Yet many of these teens struggle with issues of their faith at a very different level to their peers, who have been Christians for a relatively short time. Having been promoted through all the ranks from church crèche to children's church and now to youth church, they can explain issues such as having an intimate relationship with God in an academic way, but lack the personal experience of such intimacy which many of their newly converted friends have. Some of these long serving faithful Christians look on with jealousy, while others begin to look elsewhere.

There are those teenagers who have known Jesus since childhood and who continue to grow in their faith to a full and satisfying experience. Others look on, feeling wounded, cheated and spiritually abandoned. The new members of the group seem to be far more advanced. They have a freshness that only conversion can bring. The older believers look on, unable to relate to the conversion experience; for them being a Christian is all they have ever known. There is no actual moment they can recall when they turned from a sinful life that was separated from God, nor can they say their life has dramatically changed. For many individuals their spiritual journeys started from the moment they could understand who God was. They have never publicly renounced sin in a meeting. It has been a gradual, imperceptible change, so what they have changed from is less clear-cut. A newly-converted sixteen-year-old from an unchurched back-ground can point to a complete turn around in lifestyle: those young people brought up in the church can't do so. Their faith has grown and developed in the same way as every other part of their physical, social, mental and emotional life. Christianity focuses heavily upon adult conversion and change. This can be an experience church-discipled young people do not fully comprehend or appreciate.

As leaders we should seek to find time with those who feel like antique believers. We must talk through how they feel, whether they are growing or left struggling, and pray for ways to break the mould that holds them. In my experience with these young lifetime pew fillers, there are five main issues that prevent growth.

Is Jesus their Lord?
The most important thing to discover is whether at this moment in time they are living as his disciples, submitting to his ways and having an assurance of salvation (Acts 16:31). They may have been to every Christian mission, outreach, or concert you have taken the group to. They may have sat in every meeting where a strong appeal is given, yet never responded. We, as leaders, may assume they made a decision a long time before joining the group, or before we were on the scene, but it may well be they have never actually made a decision to follow Jesus.

Do they feel insignificant in their faith compared to others?
Many of those raised in the church scene can feel inferior around new believers who have so much enthusiasm and zeal for their faith, while they themselves don't have quite the same freshness. Nor do they have the same dramatic testimonies that speak of flirting with big fat juicy sins which have always been no-no's to the faithful long timer. Regrets can surface of never having been free to just play around. Feelings of being trapped by their 'inherited faith' can bring a creeping sense of bitterness.

Do they feel God does not love them as much as he loves other people?
Along with feelings of insecurity come the feelings not too dissimilar to the prodigal son's brother. He had never done anything wrong and yet all the attention had gone to the sinful prodigal. Did his father not love him as much as his sinful brother? Does God not love them as much as he loves the new converts – doesn't the Bible says God rejoices more over one sinner repenting rather than ninety-nine already saved? (Lk.15:7) Does he even notice their faithfulness? Feelings of rejection by God and resentment towards the new believers can develop.

Is it their actual desire to have the life God promises?
Do they genuinely want that which God has for them or have they reached the point where it is time to break away from an inherited faith? Fairly central to adolescence is the entire issue of making decisions as an individual. Young people want to prove their maturity, not accepting values imposed by others but discovering new values for themselves. Has the time come to explore elsewhere?

Are they actually walking in God's truths without realising it?
In the words of Micah 6:8: 'I have showed you, O man, what is good: and what does the Lord require of you, but to act justly, love mercy and walk humbly with your God?' It is possible that members of your group are completely unaware that they are doing the things God asks of them, walking hand in hand with their Creator, and yet feeling so much in the shadow of other believers they cannot see the fruit and depth of their own faith.

What is the answer to these young heroes, who have persevered with their faith while many of their peers have lived more worldly lives, and who are now struggling to grow? For those who have not yet submitted their lives to Jesus the solution is simple. They can either do so and experience growth, continue as they are in a stale and fruitless way or leave altogether. This decision remains on their own shoulders, as it does for anyone choosing the faith for the first time.

It is on those who fall in the other three categories that I want to concentrate: those who feel insignificant in the presence of other believers, those who feel God does not love them as much as he loves new believers, and those who are unaware they are exactly where God wants them to be. How do we raise the spiritual and emotional morale and belief of these precious people?

- Take time actively to meet with the individuals.
- Do not patronise them with Bible texts – listen to what they are saying and help them get to grips with the issues. Use the Bible wisely: it is a sword, not a club!
- Seek to encourage the young person again and again with the fact God knows about them (Ps. 139), loves them (Jer. 31:3) and wants to draw close and lavish his goodness upon them (1 Jn. 3:1).
- Point out that God looks at our heart and into our soul (1 Sam. 16:7) He knows exactly who we are and what we have done.
- Remind the young person of biblical characters such as David and Timothy. God did not despise or look down on them for their youthfulness or childhood conversion, but placed them in privileged positions. A young person open to God can be used in a powerful and mighty way, making a radical difference (1 Tim. 4:12).
- Encourage the young person to look at his or her life in detail. Ask them to make a list of what they do for God, spiritually, socially, physically and mentally (see Action page). Let them see the fruit in their lives and assure them fruit cannot grow without Jesus (Jn. 15:4,5).
- Pray with the young person that God will draw close and they will feel the assurance and value they need as well as claiming for themselves the scriptures you have read with them.
- Ask the Holy Spirit to fill them for the first time or for the hundredth time. The Holy Spirit, on encountering dry bones, breathes life and sprinkles living water for growth (Jn. 16:12–15, Rom. 8:11, Gal. 5:22–25).
- Allow them to take and retain responsibility for their long-term commitment within the group. Such maturity should be

rewarded. It will encourage the older mature Christian in their
value and the younger somewhat enthusiastic believer to see the
faithfulness of his or her peers.

Let us encourage those young people in our group to 'press on
towards the goal to win the prize for which God has called them
heavenwards in Christ Jesus' (Phil. 3:14). If for others the need to
rebel is overwhelming, don't stand in the way; in fact see it rather
as a positive part of adolescent and spiritual growth. Many of my
youth group have needed to take time out of their faith. Not
because they didn't love God but because they had to discover
themselves and discover God in a way that they might never have
done if they had remained in the rut that had ensnared them. For
some the sad reality is they may leave the faith altogether. We
must continually pray that the rich foundation they received as
children will bring them back to the truth they once knew.

Action Page

Chart of growth

Example of areas in your life where you actively do things for God

Spiritual	Social	Physical	Mental
Pray	Witness	Eat balanced food	Read my Bible

PROBLEM
How can I get members of my youth group to attend church?

Category   *Integrating young people into the church*

Symptoms   *The youth group meet outside before the service starts and stay outside until it ends, only coming in once coffee is served.*
You receive complaints because one of the young people disrupted the service by snoring loudly.
All the teenagers have united together in their request that they will only attend church when the music comes from the late 20th and not the late 18th century.

Case History
Charles has been the youth worker of St Agatha's church for the last four years. He receives a very good salary, which the church has made considerable sacrifices to find. Over the last year Charles has become increasingly aware of a growing resentment towards him. Members of the congregation are beginning to ask whether they are getting value for money. What does Charles do with his time, where are the fruits of his work? Before they employed the youth worker, the church had more young people attending than they do now. An average week now sees around five teenagers in the seats among a church of 150 adults.

When Charles hears these remarks he remains silent, not wishing to give an insulting reply. The reality is that every Sunday evening at his house, over forty young people turn up for Bible Study and in-depth prayer, but not one of them wants to come to church. If he were to reply 'They are at my house; they don't want to come to church because it's boring!' he is sure to lose his job.

Care Plans

If you were to ask the average member involved in one of the youth events you run each week, and who comes to your events but not to church, why they do not attend, the reply would in all likelihood be 'Because it is boring'.

Such an answer will come as no surprise to anyone who has any involvement at all with young people and the current youth culture. With youth churches springing up all over the place and proving to be incredibly successful, is there a place for young people in the more established churches? Can we really integrate them or is this just a dream? Should church councils sack all their youth workers and, waving flags of defeat, pack the teenagers off to the nearest youth congregation?

My experience agrees with my belief that young people can thrive spiritually in a church service that mainly focuses its attention on the older adult members of the congregation. Young people do have their own culture, tendencies and needs contrasting sharply with those of a thirty-, forty-, fifty- or sixty-year-old. However we often disregard the fact that they are young adults who are capable of adjusting to a more mature style of service and may indeed benefit by doing so.

Bridging the gap between young people and what they would describe as a terminally boring service best suited to the needs of a corpse is not something that is achieved quickly or easily. Yet if a church firmly believes in the full body of Christ (1 Cor. 12:12) being united in worship, then youth leaders, ministers, congregations and young people must struggle to achieve this. At times it will involve heated discussions and the making of compromises. It is a brave church that is willing to integrate its younger members into its life by valuing them as real members of the congregation. It is an even braver church that simply demands young people attend but makes no move to integrate them.

Steps to Integration

- Discuss the issue with the various youth groups. With a large sheet of paper, ask the group to write down constructively what in church services is a turn off for them. After what may well be an age of time, ask them to now think what is positive about the church service; what aspects they enjoy (the list may be shorter). Then ask the group what changes they would want to see in church services to make them a place where they felt happy and comfortable.

- Invite the church minister to the youth groups and ask him to share his heart for where young people, theologically, socially and practically fit into the life of the church. After listening to the minister, produce the sheet filled in at the previous meeting. Point out the negatives, positives and the areas where they would like to see change and ask the minister to comment. After his thoughts, open the floor for comments. Show your commitment to the young people by not allowing your guest to make empty promises, which are likely to remain unfulfilled.

- Review with the youth group the meeting they have had with the minister and evaluate the direction forward. Here are five radical suggestions that have proved to be effective:

  - An elected member of the group should be given a seat on the church council, deacons' or elders' meeting, with full voting rights. The voice and opinion of a young person should be heard, as well as the voice and opinion of a youth leader.

  - An elected member of the group should be given a seat on the ministry committee. If young people are to be present in the service, then leaders need to hear first-hand the thoughts and feelings of younger members.

  - Offers of youth services should be temporarily declined. Instead, push for young people to be involved and actively to take a part in the adult services. Request that willing members of the group be placed on rotas such as reading, prayers, distribution of communion and the welcoming role. Some members of the group will show real communication talents and spiritual maturity and, with time and grooming, pressure should be exerted to allow these young people to use their gifts in teaching and the leading of services.

- Encourage an open house where, once a month or so, members of the congregation are welcome to attend specific youth events. Ask also for a quarterly verbal report to be given to the congregation, explaining what has taken place recently. Request a part of the notice board for a visual and attractive display, so the congregation can be kept in touch with previous and coming events.

- Consider suggesting that the part of the youth department responsible for Bible studies and teaching (i.e. the youth fellowship) should merge with the adult house groups. It would follow a similar direction as the other house groups, while carefully maintaining its own youth identity and fulfilling its unique youth requirements.

When you begin to dig deeper into why young people loathe attending church services at times, the issue of 'Church is boring' proves to be merely a surface complaint. It cannot be denied that young people (along with many adults) dislike dreary services which, not unsurprisingly, result in a poor turnout. Dealing with this issue is not a youth-related problem but a church problem: all the members are affected. And yet many active churches, with exceptionally good communicators who make preaching something worth listening to, and which do not have particularly long services, often have exactly the same problem in keeping young people. Why?

Below the 'surface' there are two main issues which determine young people's attitude to church attendance:

- They need to belong and to play a part.
- They require identity and responsibility.

These common adolescent needs are as relevant to church life as they are to a party or a football game. Church is not just a spiritual arena: before, during and after the service it provides a gigantic social arena. Where does a thirteen-year-old fit into such an environment; what does the teenager have in common with a 45-year-old bank manager, a 70-year-old pensioner or a mother of three children?

One has to answer: 'very little'. Most of the time young people are ignored (unintentionally) and feel they do not fit into this social network. Young people mainly feel their identity is found in what they do, rather than who they are. When it comes to church they do nothing – therefore they have no identity!

The above five suggestions tackle the issues of a young person's sense of belonging, identity and responsibility within the church body. If attendance is a problem try them; they may just work!

Rather than lose young people on Sunday mornings or evenings, welcome them and use them. Allow them to be young adults in an adult environment, stimulated by the worship, the sermon and the company. Be a full body of believers with a realistic commitment to integration.

Action Page

Questionnaire

- Do 90 per cent of all young people who attend one or more of your weekly youth group activities attend church? If not, why not?

- Does the church encourage young people to attend its services?

- Does the church make active provision for integration?

- What are your young people saying about Sunday services?

- What could your church do for greater integration?

PROBLEM
How can I get my youth group to pray?

Category   *Prayer bashing*

Symptoms   *Times of prayer usually consists of gurgles and deathly silence.*
At the last prayer meeting five of the members fell asleep, two members had a snog in the corner and the rest left the room unnoticed.

Case History

It was the end of the youth meeting. As usual, the group had been very talkative, contributing whenever asked. Jill, one of the leaders, asked the group to just think about what they had heard that night. This was something she did every week and then she would invite them to spend five minutes or so in open prayer.

Jill lived in hope, because no matter how talkative or rowdy the group had been, when it came to prayer the room would go deathly silent apart from the occasional rumbling tummy and sniffing nose. Nobody ever prayed. The atmosphere always became strained: instead of five minutes of prayer, it turned into ten minutes of prolonged silence. Jill suffered in desperation, longing that someone would pray. She was convinced that if just one prayed, then the rest of the group would follow suit. After an agonising amount of time, Jill reluctantly prayed and closed the meeting. Every time the group finished she would leave disheartened. Even though it had been a good evening she could just never get them to pray.

Care Plans

I wonder how many of us have been there at one time or another, struggling with our youth groups to get a bleep out of them when it comes to prayer. Grand images of the entire group beating on the doors of heaven, slamming spiritual breeze-blocks onto the gates of hell and keeping at bay any unwanted spiritual entities, can at times seem far off. Yet surely it doesn't have to be that way. Why can't our groups be filled with spiritual giants who wage war in prayer, changing the lives of the very community they live in? Many young people are not entirely sure what prayer is, other than a list of requirements like: 'Lord, help me with my exams, I haven't revised at all', 'Lord, I've seen a really fit girl, please may she be interested in me', or: 'Lord, I need money!' So how do we get past the 'I want' or 'I need' ideas of prayer, in order to introduce them to its global and cosmic dimensions?

Many of the spiritual heroes of old have described prayer as something beyond merely the talking and listening of communication, believing it to be supremely mystical and beyond tangency. As our bodies require oxygen to keep us alive, to take into our bodies and for it to become a part of us, so prayer is to take God from the surface and bring him into our deepest part, interacting with him at the highest level available (Rev. 3:20). It is a need we have on a daily basis, knowing that to starve ourselves of such spiritual oxygen is to cut back a part of the life within us.

Explaining to a young person the importance of prayer is one thing, but when it comes to the actual 'how to', many of us are left pondering. Before we cover the 'how to', it's important that both we as leaders and the young people in our groups understand the vastness of prayer, in terms of style and resources. Below is a list of seven common aspects of prayer that a young person should be encouraged to adopt within their public and private prayer life.

- **Praise:** An expression of love in word or song (Jn. 4:23, Ps. 92:1)
- **Thanksgiving:** Acknowledging your full appreciation of what God has done (Ps. 107:1–3)

- **Repentance:** Continually humbling ourselves and asking for forgiveness for when we have fallen (1 Jn. 1:9)
- **Intercession:** To pray on behalf of others or for situations (Rom. 15:30)
- **Petition:** Giving our own needs to God and asking for his help (Matt. 7:7,8, Jn. 15:16)
- **Reflection:** To contemplate and reflect on God, his nature and his creation (Ps. 8:3–9)
- **Receiving:** Listening to God speak to us (1 Sam. 3:9)

The constant desire to raise young godly people who love the Lord with a passion extends to wanting them to have an active prayer life, one where they walk daily and intimately with God, just as the Bible describes Enoch of old (Gen. 5:24). Their experience of prayer must be positive. As leaders we should not be too shy to pray, and at all times we should create a positive praying environment within the group. This is so much easier to say than to do. How do we produce a youth group who are just wild about praying?

Firstly be committed to praying on an individual level and with other leaders for the exercise and experience of prayer in the group.

Secondly make it fun and creative.

Thirdly take time for the group to feel fully at ease with one another throughout the meeting. Plenty of interaction helps young people feel more free to express themselves when it comes to prayer.

Fourthly if it is at all possible, then include sung worship within your group, preferably before and during the time you have allocated for prayer. Aptly chosen songs with descriptive lyrics can become a great focus for prayer. A competent musician is required and the use of good lively songs helps (not dreary tunes or lyrics that make no sense). If a musician can't be found then consider using a tape, though tapes have a certain manufactured and artificial feeling, whereas a worship leader who is sensitive to the atmosphere of the group, and is present in the room at the time of the meeting is a far superior option.

It is my experience that once a group is comfortable praying then it becomes infectious. Each week you may find them begging for prayer and dissatisfied if the meeting goes on too long, cutting out the prayer time. The desire to pray with faith, believing for results, whether it be for someone who is sick, downtrodden or who doesn't know Jesus, becomes strong and enthusiastic. Taking Luke 18:1–8 as their pattern, young people will hammer away like the persistent widow until the judge (who in our case is God) grants their requests. Believing God hears them and that they can change the world they live in is enough reason to find them queuing up outside when you organise the youth prayer night.

So how can we get to the stage where prayer is number one on their agenda and how can we make prayer fun, creative and still hold onto the reverence of being in God's presence? Here is a list of ways I have used with various groups that has created the most productive praying environments. You may find some of these activities shallow but often the main barriers to prayer, such as 'speaking out loud' and 'what do I say', will be broken. Once a group is relaxed, then a more in-depth style can be adopted.

Relay prayer: Arm yourself with a stopwatch, a whistle and stick a piece of paper on the wall with a list of prayer issues written on it. Split everyone into teams, of around six or so members (the teams must be of the same size, since this is a race), and as soon as the whistle blows the teams start praying. The first person must pray for the first subject on the list, then the next person for the second subject, the third person the third subject and so on. The idea is the group who prays for the most subjects by the time the whistle blows again are that week's champion intercessors. Before deciding winners, the leaders must watch over and ensure the teams are praying sincerely and not just spouting off words.

Group prayer: In small groups everyone shares one thing they want prayer for, then the person directly opposite them prays, for no more or less than one minute

Alphabet prayer: With the whole group create a circle and explain tonight they are going to pray but this time through the alphabet, the first person must pray, using one sentence only, about anything to do with the letter 'A' e.g. 'Andrew the Church Minister' or 'Afghanistan' the next person must pray about anything to do with B, then C and on it goes until you reach Z.

Chaos prayer: With notification and themes to pray for, tell the group that after you have counted to three, they are all to pray out loud at once for a designated amount of time. This is quite an effective form of praying and can turn out to be very loud, so the neighbours need to be warned. For more shy groups, leaders must be committed to praying out loud as well. Often several leaders speaking loudly will encourage the group to follow.

Receiving prayer: With this kind of prayer ask the group to sit quite still with their eyes closed and inform them you are going to pray, asking the Holy Spirit to speak to each member in the group. Tell them, as soon as you have finished praying, to remember the very first thing that came into their head. On a sheet of paper write down exactly what strange and wonderful pictures people had slotted into their minds when you finished praying. I have done this with groups of eight to forty, and every time each person has received something entirely different. Yet as I have gone through the list, a pattern develops. This can leave your hair standing up on the back of your neck as a clear message comes across, usually related to a scripture, which is a word in season for either the whole group or members of the group. Don't be afraid if it doesn't work or you don't understand the message, it's still fun.

Newspaper prayer: Split into small groups, give each group a newspaper, then designate a theme for each group to find, for example one group to find something local, another group something national, and another something international. Ask each group to come up with one particular article they think should be prayed about. Rejoin as a large group going through the articles selected and then invite everyone (one at a time and voluntarily) to pray for the issues mentioned.

Prayer shouldn't just be left to tag on to the end of the meeting – give it real importance. When they reach that stage of being hungry for spiritual wrestling, get your group involved in additional prayer events. Try prayer concerts with other local youth groups, half night and full nights of prayer. Use special events like Christmas or Easter to do an unusual prayer gig. On Halloween I would take my group from urban London out to a countryside farm and spend the entire night praying about the issues associated with Halloween. The group would practise warfare inside and outside. The cold, the country quietness and the pitch black eerie night built the ideal atmosphere you could wish for when Halloween prayer bashing.

Another suggestion is to buy a big book and stick on the front 'Prayer journal'. Each week have someone record what was prayed for and then the next week or at the end of the month, open up the journal and go through the issues asking what became of them. Young people thrive on answered prayer, especially if things have seemed pretty grim. Not everything may be answered as we want but prayer journals are great testimonies to God and encourage persistence in prayer. When we see a direct answer to prayer, don't forget to write it in the journal. Months later it can make great reading!

Every youth group I have been involved with has struggled with prayer to start with, but with perseverance and the challenge of making it fun and creative, those youth groups have always valued prayer as the best part of the meeting. That's how it should be. Speaking about God is one thing. Meeting with him through the Bible, worship and then in intercession is something different altogether. When young people begin to pray, youth groups change for good!

PROBLEM
How do I deal with teenage self-esteem?

Category   *Teenage Blues*

Symptoms   *You discover the bottle of wine and anti-depressants being passed around the room in the middle of Fellowship group.*
Your office becomes a psychiatric clinic after school for all those who have the 'I hate life' blues or 'I'm in love but she doesn't love me syndrome'.

Case History

He knew it wasn't going to be easy, going into school today. Carl was the school chaplain and he had received a phone call informing him a pupil from the school had committed suicide by taking an overdose. When he heard the name of the pupil a cold sensation shivered through his body. 'Jane Trent' said the headmaster, on the other end of the phone. This was a deep blow for the chaplain. Jane had been his star pupil in RE. Not only had she started the Christian Union single-handed, but also, because of her attractive personality and strong convictions, it had grown to over fifty members. Jane had made her faith very public. She had asked if she could lead assemblies and have lunch debate clubs. Permission had been given for both, and most pupils from each year knew of Jane and liked her.

Carl was given the job of taking the special assembly announcing the news to the entire school. In front of some eight hundred pupils, he slowly and carefully broke the news. Not wanting to be long winded he just made one real point '... as you know Jane was a good friend of mine and many of you. She made it very clear she was a Christian and her faith was her strength. It's very hard to say what happened or even what she was thinking. Some of you are asking 'Where was God for her last night?' I guess in a way Jane had swum out to sea, and begun to go under the water. The deeper and deeper she went, the smaller and further the sun seemed to be as she looked up from the depth of the water. Eventually, she reached a point where the sun was so small and seemed so unreachable, it was easier to give up'. With tears in his eyes he paused for a moment and with great restraint continued 'But my dear Jane, the sun hadn't stopped shining and it hadn't gone away!'

Care Plans

Just for a moment, think back to when you last heard someone in your group say: 'I'm so depressed!' Most likely it wasn't so long ago. Teenagers and depression seem to go hand in hand, usually a reaction to a sad situation such as the break up of a relationship, the separation of parents, failing an exam, not making the team in sports, falling out with a best friend, the death of a family member, or not getting one's first choice of sixth form college or university. In most cases we think nothing of it, we just offer our support and encouragement and eventually in time they are full of life again, and bounce right back into things. Crisis over!

Adolescence is a rocky stage at the very best of times, and when extra stresses are thrown into the melting pot such as

- high expectations,
- lack of parental support or understanding,
- media pressures e.g. must be attractive, blond, busty (female) or anorexically thin,
- peer pressures to conform in areas where the individual is not comfortable,
- relationship pressures such as sex or having to make compromises,
- avoiding being mediocre or just OK at something as it's seen as failure; who wants to be average?

- parental separation,
- financial independence.

then the individual's sense of value and self worth takes an all-time dip. With these stresses and the pressures of today's society, young people are indeed at risk of the blues, clinical depression and thoughts or stronger feelings towards suicide.

The problem we face as youth leaders in recognising the vulnerable and bruised members of our group is that adolescent behaviour generally covers up real depression. It's hardly abnormal for a young person to be bouncing all over the place one day and the next day silently moody or aggressive. Are they struggling with a specific issue or are they just being knocked about by those wild hormonal feelings?

There can be some give-away signs. Common ones to watch out for are
- Total loss of interest in things they once held dear, such as sports, hobbies, friends and food.
- A noticeable withdrawal from people, pets and basically anything that can get close to them.
- Drop in general appearance and school grades.
- Intense problems in getting the young person away from the TV, and then out of bed in a morning.
- Being locked in another world where things don't distract.
- Change in weight and general mood behaviour.

Teenagers are struggling to be exactly what they are supposed to be, young people. With society's expectations and the pace of life changing so rapidly, adolescents often fail to keep up. Many young people just cannot cope with the changes within them and around them; others struggle to surface above the rubbish dumped on them in the shape of a family divorce or the death of a close relative or friend.

It's our role not just to be there, but to notice. Sometimes it's not hard to read the signs of abnormal behaviour such as cutting oneself, habitual drinking, sleeping around, going through relationships like the change of weather, a major loss of or gain in weight, dropping out of fellowship group and church. Sometimes more subtle signs may escape us. But always remember the core issue in youth work is relationships. Always make sure each of your young people has one leader to whom they can relate, one who gives them more than a casual 'Hello, how was school this week?' Have leaders who reach beyond the superficialities and who are able to sense the deeper areas of concern in the young person and to encourage them to share these. When leaders know young people, they can tell the difference between a mood swing and something out of the ordinary, while casual observers would not notice. They will know much more about what's happening in their life, what the state of play is at home, in school, and be aware of the individual's self-image and self-esteem.

What else should a responsible youth leader do?
Always take an interest in each individual member of the group.
I had two youth leaders through my time. The first leader could never remember my name, even though there were only ten in the group. After eight weeks of repeatedly asking who I was, I figured I was of no value or importance to that leader. The second leader in a different group (of around thirty members), not only knew my name, but remembered my birthday, noticed when I had new shoes, hair cut, clothes. Whatever it was she noticed. Along with every other member of that group, I felt valued and important!

Always take time to find out how they are doing, and what they are doing.
Divide your leaders so you can meet members of your group outside of church activities on their own or neutral ground, such as McDonald's, at a sports event they are involved in, or at the cinema with a film they want to see. It doesn't matter what, just show you are committed and interested.

Always encourage and build individuals up.
Some may not know how to cope with the positive affirmation and be sarcastic (don't worry, keep on praising them.) Some will

just revel in it. Regardless of which they may be, the message will be heard, received and it will bless them.

Always let the group know not only are they loved by you but they are also loved by God.
Tell them in every possible way, from every possible angle, what the Bible says. Read chapters like Psalm 139, Isaiah 40–43, Jeremiah 31:3, John 3. Read the love songs, the statements of Jesus, and the New Testament letters, with their implications. Let them just fall into the secure arms of the one who loves them faithfully and unconditionally.

In hard and difficult times always draw close to them.
Reassure them, watch them carefully; let them know of your commitment to them and how much you value them. Pray with them, speak Bible passages into their lives such as Psalm 46:1 'God is our refuge and strength, an ever-present help in trouble' or Psalm 139 on how he watches over us and knows what we face.

If it appears that their own safety is not secure in their own hands or their depression has reached new depths, refer them to home and parents, or, if home is not safe then encourage them to go to a GP – offer to go with them. If that fails, then without hesitation contact Social Services, explaining your concerns and fears, with any additional information you may have. Tell the young person any action you may take and why. The story of Jane is not an isolated incident – teenage suicide, regardless of faith, is on the increase. Just under half of all teens consider suicide at one time or another.

Let's protect our young people, understand them, love them, encourage and support them. Let us give them the security and true identity to grow into mature adults, with the positive images they should have of themselves. What a fantastic opportunity we have of turning negative images into positive ones, helping them to see truths about themselves that they'll remember for the rest of their lives!

Action Page

It is important that when we deal with young people who are low, depressed, in need of help and advice that we know what we are doing. Below are eighteen guidelines recommended by Youth for Christ. These are not rules for the sake of having rules. They are there to protect you and the person you are dealing with.

- Always talk and pray with someone in a group of more than two, if at all possible. One-to-one contact may take place only in a public place (and your supervisor should agree if it becomes necessary to continue).
- Always counsel with the same sex – i.e. two males with a male, two females with a female, when involved in praying with young people. If this is impossible, then you should counsel in a public place, with the agreement of your supervisor.
- Always talk and pray in an open space where others are around: privacy is a factor but don't go alone.
- Confidentiality is vital – they will need to know that you will not go to others and talk about their problems. However, do not promise to keep a secret. You may need to tell someone in authority. If that is so, tell them who it will be and what you will say – in order to build trust.
- Keep calm and be honest. Don't feel you have to know all the answers. If you don't know, find someone who does and ask them.
- Don't be afraid to ask for advice. We are not here to prove anything to anyone, we want the best for the young people in our care. If you feel out of your depth or unsure, ask someone to help you.
- Don't keep bringing the conversation round to your experience, i.e. 'I remember when that happened to me and I . . .'. Testimony is good, but listen.
- Don't make promises you can't keep.
- Don't appear shocked or appalled.
- Be sensitive, don't say things like – 'I can't believe it – why didn't you tell anyone before?'

- Don't laugh at them.
- Don't minimise or trivialise the issues, even if they may not seem important to you. If they need to talk about it, it is important.
- Be aware of your body language, the way you are reacting. Always encourage and affirm, don't judge or condemn.
- Don't feel you have to wrap it up straight away: some things need more talking through. Discuss it with a leader or prayer co-ordinator. Don't offer to do it on your own, or offer the availability of someone else before checking it out with them.
- If you are told about anything illegal you must tell your supervisor, or their delegated representative, straight away. However, at the time of print, there is no general legal duty to report an offence to the police.
- Don't take on board other people's problems as if they were your own. Remember, empathy is standing in someone else's shoes, with your feet firmly in your own.
- Do not under any circumstances touch someone inappropriately when praying or talking with them. Avoid issues such as hugging – whether same sex or opposite sex. Remember we need to be above reproach.
- Follow up check how they are doing the following week.

If you are in agreement with the above guidelines as a sensible and safe act, and you have not already taken on board similar guidelines, commit yourself to using them each time you counsel and pray with a young person.

I .... (name) agree to the above guidelines and wish to restrict myself to its recommendations.

Signed ....   Date ....

PROBLEM
Is the media and the music world of the Devil?

Category   *Young people, media and culture*

Symptoms   *After going to watch an action film at the cinema, members of your group are caught setting fire to the church choir stalls.*
A new satanic church called 'The Corner Café' is stealing members of your flock as it plays MTV instead of singing hymns.

Case History

It was the end of the mission. Some twenty-five young people had made real decisions to turn and follow Jesus. Now we had them, we didn't really know what to do with them. We nervously took them to church the next Sunday, wondering if they would stay in for more than five minutes. They sat before the service, somewhat fidgety, looking around asking questions such as 'Why did we have a cross hanging on the wall?', 'Isn't that a bit morbid?' and, 'Why does the geezer at the front wear a dress?'

As leaders we sat feeling more tense by the moment, sensing they were just too raw as believers to ever survive a real service. Then the celebration started, the band struck up at the front and launched into a song. Each and every one of the new Christians sat up in their seats and began to chat among themselves. 'This is it' I thought, 'We have already lost control'. Eventually the hardest and toughest character of them all turned with a smile on his face and said 'It's all right this, isn't it! A bit trendier than I reckoned'. The music that morning gripped those new believers and as time went by it brought them into a place of worship we had never anticipated.

Care Plans

Having a job that necessitates travel, I have come to realise (what many already know) that although the universal language may be English, among young people it is truly music. Whether in California, London, Moscow or Manila, young people speak this language fluently and are equally influenced by it.

One of the most common questions I am asked by leaders is whether music and the media are harmful to the all-too-eager young eyes and ears that freely allow whatever is available to enter their heads? At the risk of sounding like a spiritual killjoy, my answer to such a question is: 'It depends what they are watching or listening to'.

The reality is that much of the music world is far from wholesome. Explicit lyrics about sex or the implications of it, the endorsement of drugs and glorifying of violence and the occult can all be found in the charts, week in, week out. Think of the most recent box office blockbuster films. How many of them have been devoid of sex, violence, twisted horror or severe bad language? I can think of very few.

Even TV adverts can be suggestive, using lustful images to invite you to buy their products. When you ask the average conscientious Christian young person about this, the usual response is: 'I don't listen to the music for the lyrics, I just like the tune'. When it comes to films the answers are not much different 'I just ignore those parts'.

Every time I hear such a reply I genuinely believe the individual, but I doubt the lyrics go by without making some impression. We are all influenced by what we hear and see. Several best-selling teenage magazines make no secret of the fact they cover issues such as: 'How to have an affair with a married man', or: 'How to sexually satisfy your boy friend'. Even if the young person would never do such a thing, new thoughts have been planted that were not present before.

The Bible does not condone such idle reading, listening to or watching corrupt and ungodly things. Instead, it instructs us to consider whatever is pure, whatever is noble and whatever is good and to think on these things. (Phil. 4:8). Romans 12:2 urges us not to conform to the patterns of this world but to be transformed by the renewing of our minds. With images of sex, violence and corruption plaguing our thoughts as we relax and enjoy a film, read a magazine or listen to a song, it isn't easy for our minds to be transformed in the way St. Paul urges us. Jesus suggests the truth is in the action: 'The good man brings good things out of the good stored within him'. (Mt. 12:35) The question is, are we in danger of storing bad things within if we get our entertainment from such sources? And is it really a danger as long as we don't communicate to others what we see and hear? If we answer 'no' to the second question we are really saying it doesn't matter what we watch.

Many churches have actively tried to help young people in this whole area by banning attending the cinema or listening to secular music. This certainly tackles the issue head-on. The responsibility is then taken out of the hands of the young person, but I wonder whether it is the best solution available. Adolescence is about learning and developing, and if such strong restrictions are imposed on something so fundamental to a young person's culture, we are not helping them to decide what is right or wrong. Much of the media, in my opinion, does not fit into the absolute categories that we can make quick judgments about, such as sex outside marriage, drugs and alcohol abuse. It would be wrong and misleading to suggest all music is corrupt, all films are evil and all magazines are perverted because this is not the case. There is much good material available for young people to digest and be influenced by in the media and music culture.

We should allow our young people responsibility in this matter, having first explained biblically the issues at stake, and why there is such a concern from a Christian angle. This should be accompanied with an emphasis on the rightness of listening, reading and watching good, pure and noble things within the media and music world. When young people are given permission to act responsibly, they are more likely to make right choices than when they are given no choice other than to disobey. We should say 'no' sparingly and be creative when approaching difficult issues.

Let us then as leaders be aware of what our young people are facing and dealing with; let us give positive, sensible and realistic guidance. Protect them from spiritually negative influences and impurities but carefully avoid dictating to them: 'do this' or 'don't do that'. When it comes to the media and young people we must remember that Christian young people should not be 'of the world', yet they are living in it. To cut them off entirely from the media and its message is to separate them from the reality of today's world and nearly every friend they have. The media has a role to play in the development of our young people – let us seek out the good that it has to offer as well as guarding against the bad.

PROBLEM
I think I'm in love with a member of my youth group!

Category   *Burning desires*

Symptoms   *Can't keep your eyes off the beauty in the corner.*
You only listen to the point made and accept answers from the Golden Goddess.
Always keen to offer him or her a lift home alone.
When she looks at you, you lose it completely, dreaming of snogs in the park.

Case History

Jane was only fifteen but she had the physical appearance of a nineteen- or twenty-year-old lady. Her features were striking, her hair was long and golden. Jane had the personality that could warm the hardest of hearts, and with a smile that highlighted her pearl white teeth she had no problem getting whatever she wanted. Few boys didn't stop to look twice as Jane passed by. It wasn't something she minded: she enjoyed every boy in her class swarming around her. Paul, the church youth leader, was no exception to Jane's fan club. He was twenty-three years old and very good looking. At first he didn't realise he spent more time with this young golden goddess than with any other member of his youth group. As time went on, he came to realise he was in fact physically attracted to her, and the rapport he had created was more flirtatious than was expected of a youth leader in his professional capacity.

She was constantly on his mind. He found himself not only giving her preferential treatment but inviting her to do privileged things which meant he often ended up alone with her. The response from Jane seemed to imply she was positively interested. Paul knew his feelings were wrong but was sure nothing would ever come of them; he would merely enjoy the fun of the relationship. Gradually, Paul found himself feeling more serious about the situation. There was a greater intensity and, though he dare not admit it, she was on his mind in an unhealthy way.

After dropping her home one night, Jane thanked him, smiled and gave him a long glance. Paul seeing it as an invitation could no longer contain himself. He lent across to kiss her. She did not stop him, nor did she return the kiss in any way. Then Paul reached across and placed his hand upon her. Jane immediately froze. Paul, somewhat embarrassed, removed his hand. But it was too late: no words were said and Jane left the car in silence.

A couple of weeks later the fifteen-year-old arranged a meeting with the church minister and told him about the entire situation. The police were involved and Paul was asked to step down from leadership.

Thirteen years later, Jane pursued the situation again. This time she tried to sue the church for compensation, as well as pursuing sexual abuse charges against Paul. The former youth worker admitted his act and was punished by the law. The church escaped compensation fees, but the judge expressed his disapproval at the lack of support offered to Jane at the time, by the congregation of this small church. Jane, now in her very late twenties, sold the story to both national and local newspapers and the church was named and shamed within the community.

Care plans

Such sad stories have wider repercussions. The damage caused from such a relatively small incident affected many people. Was Paul completely to blame, did Jane lead him on, should the church have acted differently?

Paul cannot be blamed for what he felt but the danger could have been avoided if he had followed sensible guidelines. We can all point a smug finger at Paul and say 'Silly boy', but yet we have to point the finger back at ourselves and say this could easily be any of us. There but for the precious grace of God go I. We are all human and tempted. If we are being honest, we would have to admit that almost none of us are immune from spotting hunks and beauty queens in our groups, even though most of us might say with confidence that 'it could never happen to me'. While one would not question the integrity or belief of the individual making that statement the reality of it should be questioned. Suppose a drop-dead gorgeous teenager, at the peak of their physical glory, shows an unusual attraction towards you, and you happen to be vulnerable at the time. You decide to ignore the signs and enjoy the developing friendship. Be warned: you could soon be facing the end of your career, and potentially facing charges, particularly if the person involved is a minor. Such incidents can rarely be swept under the carpet.

It's no longer unheard-of for church youth leaders or full time pastors, married and in their late twenties or early thirties, to leave their wives and families for a girl in their Bible study group. The casualties in ministry are heavy. We find ourselves in risky environments every week. We often ignore sensible guidelines because we don't have the backup of staff of the opposite sex. We may feel the rules are just too restricting or we naively think: 'It will never happen to me'.

We should prayerfully adhere to sound moral guidelines in this area, which is a dangerous one. We have to remember

- We have been given a place of responsibility. People trust us. The parents trust us, the congregation or school trusts us, the minister trusts us, and, if we're married, our partners trust us. Though the young person may be willing for a relationship or an affair to develop, they trust us and sees our actions as the right actions. Yet most of all, we have been placed in that position because God has trusted us. He specifically says: 'Do not cause one of these little ones to stumble'. (Matt. 18:5–6).
- Without guidelines we open ourselves to misunderstandings. We may be giving signals unintentionally to a member of our group, for example always being willing to give lifts home. It may be practical because they live very close to us, yet it could

be perceived differently. Too many leaders have been accused of things they didn't do, because they did not protect themselves by adhering to sensible guidelines. Young teenagers have active imaginations and are capable of passionately describing something to others as if it really happened, especially if they can't get the real thing. If we are often alone in the car with them whose story will be believed, ours or that of a fourteen-year-old? Even if we are believed, there will always be an element of doubt.

- Though others may trust us, we should not be so bold as to trust ourselves. We don't have to be perverts to be attracted to a seventeen- or eighteen-year-old girl or boy who is serious about us. No one would suggest that we are going to throw ourselves on any vulnerable and attractive member of our group, but we may stumble at the subtlety of an emerging so-called harmless friendship.
- It should be realised that some people are attracted to anyone with power or authority. There is a great danger in counselling someone of the opposite sex, because emotions can get out of hand and the couple may easily fall in love with disastrous consequences. This is often referred to by counsellors as 'transference'.

Healthy Guidelines

It is our role to preserve and to protect. Having a relationship with a young person in our care, in any capacity other than leader and friend is abusing our position. In Philippians 1:27 Paul urges us to conduct our lives in a manner worthy of the Gospel. We should periodically take a check on all our relationships and, with the aid of the Holy Spirit and our conscience, examine each of them to see if it is being conducted in such a manner. We may not take lightly the words of Jesus when he spoke about causing the little ones to stumble. Who are the little ones Jesus speaks about; just children? Or does he include impressionable young people looking to their leaders for direction and understanding?

It is important to point out that having feelings for a young person isn't necessarily wrong – it's what you do with those feelings that can be wrong, or can turn into something wrong. Ask God to help you with what you feel and restrict your actions with necessary guidelines. If need be, talk to someone you trust and invite them continually to ask you what is happening, what you are feeling and how you are acting on those feelings. You may not wish to share with a leader as they may act impulsively, but your mentor must have the right to share their doubts about you to your superior if you do not act responsibly. Leaders have failed and of course there is forgiveness, but though we can be forgiven failure has its cost. Let us avoid failure therefore, be responsible and show good reason why others have confidence in us and our ministry. A restrictive ministry is a sensible ministry.

Action page

The seven easy steps to stay safe with an attractive youth group.

- Never counsel a member of the opposite sex if at all possible. If you really have to, because you have no opposite sex leaders, then do it with another member of staff. Use a room with other people in it, so all can see but not hear.
- Never be alone with members of the opposite sex. Leave the door open at all times for people to see.
- Do not take a member of the opposite sex home in the car alone. Make sure you drop off the member of your sex last.
- If hugging is fine in your group make sure it is appropriate. Don't be physical in any other way, e.g. don't allow the fourteen-year-old girls to jump all over the twenty-two-year-old male leaders. This is often not as innocent as it can appear.
- Make sure your actions are never suggestive or flirtatious. For example, maybe members of the youth group are saying how Jenny has put on weight. Wanting to support Jenny and her feelings you may say 'Jenny, you have a lovely figure'. What's wrong with that? Nothing! But Jenny may see it as a flirtatious remark.
- Treat each member of the group equally. Watch yourself and make sure you're not giving more attention to any one person, especially one of the opposite sex.
- Check your heart often: 'Do I feel anything for this person, am I showing special treatment, am I keen to be alone with them, do I feel more for them than anyone else?' If you are unsure or cannot say a definite 'no' then be strong and firm in your actions. Don't do anything that would break the above guidelines.

If you agree with the need to be restrictive and hold to strong guidelines for a safe ministry then sign below to say you vow to uphold these seven points, how ever difficult it may be.

From this day .... (date) I .... (name) will ensure I keep at all time to the seven recommendations above.

I believe in the need to protect myself and the young people I work with. God and other people have entrusted young people into my care and I will therefore act as a responsible and careful leader at all times.

Sign . . . .

*If, as a leader and in a position of responsibility, you are aware that you hold some form of sexual feelings for those of the same sex as you, then you should apply the same caution for young people of your sex, where above it currently specifies the opposite sex.

PROBLEM
When is sex right?

Category   *Young people, sex and relationships*

Symptoms   *The game of passing the balloon under the chin was not supposed to end up in a gigantic kissing session. The associate youth pastor thought it was a good idea to issue all couples in the group with condoms just in case things in private got out control. With summer fast approaching, the girls seemed to wear less and less until they attended group virtually naked, increasing the male attendance and conversions to an all time high.*

Case History

Bill, the youth leader of a small rural church, phoned up Karen's mother after hearing the sixteen-year-old was heading off on holiday to Ibiza with her eighteen-year-old boyfriend. Karen had not seen the contradiction between going on holiday with her non-Christian boyfriend and her faith in God. If Bill could not get through to Karen, he would try her mother.

Mrs O'Connor was happy to listen to Bill. After he had finished expressing his 'conservative' views, as Karen's mother called them, she went on to say: 'I am paying for the holiday. Of course they will have sex. That's the whole point! I have seen Karen develop quicker than most girls: she has a boyfriend she loves, and to be honest I would rather she lost her virginity in style than in the back of a dirty car. It would be nice if she waited like I did until she was married, but that's not life any more, is it? People don't wait'. With that Mrs O'Connor thanked Bill for his concern and put the phone down.

Care Plans

'What's wrong with having sex?' This is the question most young people in our youth groups want to have answered. Why is it we youth leaders stand between young people and their having that most enjoyable time? Are we just twisted killjoys? Have we actually ever thought the issue through to the point of questioning whether sex before marriage could possibly be right in certain circumstances? Rather than always being on the defensive when it comes to the issue, let's stop and analyse whether we have all the facts in place.

The 'sex before marriage is right' argument

• Sex is natural. For an adolescent at the peak of sexual development, the need to be satisfied reaches an all time high. It is a driving force that sends them chasing, begging and drooling over the opposite sex. After a snog with their boy or girlfriend, the most natural thing in the world would be to slip off their clothes and enjoy each other at the most intimate level possible.

• The media promotes it. When a teen turns on the TV, sex is often either hinted at, or graphically shown. In one way or other young people are given messages on sex continually by the media. You don't have to see a boob, bum or silky black underwear, so readily available after 9 p.m. on most channels, to conjure up pictures in your head. At 5pm you can see soaps with such scenes as a young couple kissing and then hand in hand going into another room (assumed to be the bedroom) closing the door behind them. It doesn't take much to imagine what is taking place, nor the message being given. The media is simply expressing the desires of humankind. And what is wrong with that? After all it is one of the most compelling desires we have. The lesson from the media is not to sit idle, allowing the peak of one's desire to pass one by. Life is too short to get frustrated, sex is great – enjoy!

- Society encourages it. There is a growing trend for people to marry in their thirties rather than in their twenties, and then often only if they wish to have children. With the number of divorces constantly increasing, more and more people are afraid of the commitment marriage represents. The moral boundaries have moved, and society teaches that people should be as sexually experienced as possible as a preparation for that ultimate marital relationship. It also teaches that they should discover just how sexually compatible they are with another before entering into any kind of commitment (either marriage or living together). When you do find someone who you may be interested in, then they must satisfy you, both in and out of bed, before you even consider becoming Mr and Mrs Right. You have to admit it does sound both plausible and sensible.

So it is 'sensible' on the grounds that it's natural, the media promotes it and society encourages it. Do you buy that? If you don't, remember the majority of young people do! The reality is, if one wants something strongly enough, then it can be justified. Let's be honest: the tidal wave of sexual desires and lust is a mighty strong wave. As we stand there with Bible in one hand, wagging the forefinger of the other, declaring it to be wrong, stopping that wave isn't going to be easy. Why should we want to stop it in the first place? And why are we so sure sex outside of marriage is wrong? How is it we just can't move with the times?

The 'sex outside of marriage is wrong' argument
- God created us with sexual desires, to enjoy each other at the most pleasurable level possible, to be able to go beyond the level of mere friendship at which we normally engage with others. Having love demonstrated and experienced physically makes an incredibly powerful physical and emotional bond between two people. In God's absolute wisdom though, he placed conditions on such experiences, explaining that it was for the marriage bed only. Not two intimate lovers who have been together for years, neither for two people who intend to

get married, but for two lovers who are married, because in sex they are united together. (Gen. 2:24. 1 Cor. 7:2)

- God created sex as the means for two married lovers to become one (Gen. 2:24). A bonding takes place between two people while having sex, emotionally, physically and spiritually. Such is the amazing power of this act that it knits people together, to strengthen their relationship. To have frequent casual sex or even to have had sex with only two partners means you have been joined together and become one with two or more people. The consequences are destructive, and this gift of uniting two people is seriously abused.
- Sex is to be shared between two people for life. God did not intend that we should begin to look elsewhere for gratification when the spice has gone from the relationship, but that this sacred gift should be kept within the marriage (Heb. 13:4, Matt. 19:6). Sex is a gift that generates spice.
- Sex is for procreation, to have a family (Gen. 9:1). Society today sees nothing wrong with children being born outside of marriage. Many children are in households with several siblings who all have different parents. Family life, as it is encouraged in the Bible, means having one father and one mother who are married.
- To 'go where no man or woman has been before' is sacred and supposed to be that way. If someone has shared themselves with three people or twenty people, then when that one special partner comes along it's hardly special for that chosen individual. For in the back of his or her mind will be thoughts of 'Were the others better than I am? Was it more satisfying with someone else? Would they rather be with them when it comes to sex and just have me for normal out-of-bed living?' The love bed was not designed for rivalry but for passionate intimacy between two faithful and innocent lovers.

The argument that sex is solely for the marriage relationship and not for casual or even long-term relationships outside marriage is very unpopular today. However, if we are to be biblical and faithful to God's word then we must speak out. So when it comes to explaining the issues of sex and Christian life-styles how can we talk about it without becoming tongue-tied and yet live to survive another day?

The sex guide

- It should only be shared with the most amazing partner you will ever find on the planet, your wife or husband.
- Sex is good. It's to be enjoyed, and you can have it in abundance, as much as you and your partner can physically take.
- Sex is not something to consider as wrong or negative in any way. If used as the Creator intended, then it is nothing short of wonderful.
- It should only be enjoyed and experienced within marriage.
- It unites people together. It was not intended for more than one partner.
- To have one or more sexual partners before you find the man or woman of your dreams is destructive and potentially harmful to you, your sexual partner and your future wife or husband.
- Sex within marriage can be used for the purpose of having children.
- Sex within marriage with one life partner will be free from sexually transmitted diseases. Sex with someone who has had one or more other partners already puts you at risk of contracting diseases. Some of these will stay with you for life and be passed on to your eventual husband or wife – not the nicest wedding present!
- Sex is ultimately a present from God that will bless you and your spouse and will give you an abundance of pleasure that will last throughout your lives together.

Once we have managed to explain sex as it's meant to be and have just won the 'killjoy of a lifetime' award, we need to be real about how difficult it is for teenagers in today's world, with its increasing pressure on them to have casual sex. Their sexual drive button can't just be turned off or short-circuited. Many of their peers will have sexual experience, and will brag about it in detail. The young person isn't going to find it easy to turn a deaf ear to the message of the media, and is likely to have very different ideas in the heat of passion with a drop-dead gorgeous boy or girlfriend.

So if we are going to say no, then we must also help them. Otherwise all we do is to make them feel incredibly guilty when they do get out of their depth. Below is a guide to healthy relationships.

Relationship Guide

- Encourage couples to regularly pray together.
- Any romantic relationship should be known about (e.g. parents should at least have been told by their child).
- Emphasise that only by going out with another Christian can you hope to guarantee that both hold the same values. This is the best way of ensuring that pressure will not be applied to have sex outside marriage – although it is not unknown amongst Christians, and going out with a Christian does not mean that there will never be any pressure to have sex before marriage.
- Explain good boy/girl friend relationship should not become exclusive but they should continue to meet with others and remain both sociable and visible. That doesn't mean they can't have privacy. But does stop them becoming so exclusive their only social outlook on life is each other.
- Kissing is fine but explain that long periods of passionate kissing may not be helpful, since although nice they are extremely sexually stimulating and build up immense pressure that may lead into other forms of sexual foreplay, and even the full-blown act.
- Using fingers to explore each other's bodies and the actual handling of genitals should be a definite 'no-no' since both are preludes to going 'all the way' and things become increasingly difficult to stop.
- Encourage boy/girl friends to find alternative private space other than the bedroom. If this is the only place available for them to talk in private, they should leave the door open (it goes without saying that there must be others in the house) and keep all four feet on the ground! It is also wise to avoid kissing in bedrooms. A highly arousing kissing session in the right environment could so easily lead to other things.

- Explain carefully that they should dress moderately, showing consideration for others in their choice of clothes. Today's fashions of short, tight and revealing clothes may well cause one's partner more excitement than was really intended. Look good but avoid being sexually stimulating.

As a young person I remember laughing at similar rules, vowing I would never make such legalistic guidelines. Now with the experience of having been in teenage relationships, feeling the heat and the pressures and knowing friends and fellow-members of youth groups who failed (with children to show for it), I can more than see the wisdom of such advice. If you present similar rules, don't expect all of them to be obeyed. It doesn't matter if some of the minor points are ignored because they are only warning signs. There is always an element of distance after the sign, before the danger impacts. However if young people don't have warning signs and places where they can slightly push the boundaries, they may well fall straight into the danger without realising it is there.

Some parents and churches actively speak against teenagers having a boy or girlfriend till they are seventeen or eighteen, and I can understand and strongly respect this view. However, my own experience of such a rule is that if the young person does find someone, then they are likely to have a secret relationship. It's better to know about it and have an open dialogue with them. They are far more likely to stay within the boundaries of the guidelines if the relationship is public, talked about and visible than if it is a secret relationship without guidelines.

Our commitment to young people is to raise them in the best possible way to love and obey God in every aspect of their lives, including their sexual desires. The reality is that some members may well fail, despite good intentions – the wrong place and just a little too much passionate heat resulting in an unrestrained sexual act. The young couple's action is quite understandable, but sin is sin! The most important thing we can do is offer help in getting them back on the right path, with the full forgiveness Jesus offers all his children. Sex with someone outside marriage is wrong but it's not the vilest of offences. There is forgiveness. As youth workers, we need to be impartial when someone has failed, not judgmental but approachable, loving and caring. It's more important to look to the future than dwell on the past.

Talking about sex never proves to be a silent affair. Wherever it's discussed, people feel passionately about it and are not willing to modify their sexual behaviours without being given persuasive reasons. The Biblical message is not modern or popular but it does make absolute sense!

PROBLEM
How do I deal with that teenage crush?

Category *The 'I love that really fit youth leader' syndrome*

Symptoms *You keep receiving comments about what a cute bum you have.*
You develop a new shadow though it doesn't resemble the shape of your body.
Constant tacky presents like teddy bears and love hearts arrive.
Sudden overwhelming feelings of claustrophobia.

Case History

Dave was late for an assembly and was rushing to get to the hall. He hadn't even noticed he was being followed until she called out his name. Dave turned round, to see a sixth form girl behind him. 'Hello' he said politely. That was not a good move and she didn't beat around the bush. Rapidly, she told Dave how good looking he was and how she would like to do certain things with him. Dave was running late and didn't really take in what she said. He replied: 'Not now, I'm late for an assembly!' It was only afterwards that he fully realised what she had said, and what a ridiculous reply he had given. Dave had simply not wanted to be rude, having to rush off. Yet his response only added fuel to the fire.

Her name was Diana, and Dave unfortunately bumped into her nearly every time he came to the school. It was as if she knew his every move. Each time, she expressed her feelings, and the level and intensity of what she had in mind for the two of them increased. At first he thought she was having a laugh and was picking on the school Bible basher as a bit of fun. After a time, Dave came to see it wasn't harmless fun at all but serious feelings. He began to avoid her, repeatedly telling her that he was married and simply not interested. Yet it seemed that it wasn't going in. She told him she was willing to have an affair and keep it all quiet. Things began to feel very ugly. He had no idea where this was leading or what scandal could spin from it. All Dave knew was he wasn't interested. In the end his consistent firmness killed her passion. He was a free and comfortable married man again.

Care Plans

Every teenager in the world has a crush on an older person at one time or other, and it's absolutely normal. As a youth leader, it is more than likely going to happen to you at least once, and the older they are the more serious it can become. Dealing with crushes is very important. Most crushes are not like the experience Dave had above, and often you won't even know about them. Usually it is nothing more than a sweet twelve-year-old girl who goes bright red when you talk to her. Or a fourteen-year-old boy who drops some flirtatious hints. Yet your response can make a young person sob their heart out for nights on end – or encourage them to think there is a mutual interest.

On the other hand, the knowledge that someone has a crush on you may be forced upon you by one of their friends, often in an embarrassing manner or at the wrong time. The information you just don't want is delivered in a public meeting. You are teaching in a school class room or in the middle of Bible study, and you're asking for feedback from questions related to God. Instead you are informed that you have an admirer, who thinks you're 'the most gorgeous thing on legs'.

When you discover that someone actually finds you attractive (other than your husband or wife, if you're married) don't go mad about it; get it into perspective. It's probably someone at least half your age and who probably fancies his or her maths teacher, as well – the one with the facial features of a gold fish. Blushing is uncontrollable, but doesn't help especially if you do it in front of forty young people who all find the situation absolutely hilarious. Simply brush over it. Don't respond and don't change your attitude to that person. Some leaders, when they find they have an admirer, subconsciously start flirting with the individual. Watching someone in their thirties flirting with an eleven-year-old is bizarre. It's not that they have any other agenda: they have just been flattered by the news and are grateful to have an admirer. Forget it! Others are unable to handle the news and ignore the young person to the point of exclusion. Neither of these responses is helpful nor are they the right thing to do.

Crushes do not need fuelling but putting out. Simply do not respond, remain exactly the same leader you were before to them, and it should pass over a period of time. Only if they stick to you like a leech and start to make things uncomfortable, should you make it perfectly clear you are not interested and don't want the attention you are receiving. If at all possible, ask another leader whom they trust to tell them gently they should look elsewhere, preferably someone of their own age.

If the crush comes from a seventeen-year-old, then it will come with more weight and passion. Ignore it to start with. Tell another leader what you have noticed, so they are watching your back and can pull you up if you give the wrong vibes. If things become more intense: for example, if you receive gifts, letters and phone calls, then inform them in a gentle but unmistakable way you are not interested. If need be, have the other leader tell them as well. Be sensible and avoid being alone with them.

Remember that teenagers have feelings that come and go like the wind. They will appreciate it if you don't break their hearts by being overly brutal, or by making fun of them in front of their friends. Be that really cool youth leader who understands sensitivity and tact (Prov. 16:23). If at all possible, simply wait for their feelings to change, as they eventually will.

Action Page

 A quick summary for dealing with that teenage crush

- Ignore it.
- Ask another leader to watch your back.
- Do not change your behaviour towards them in any way (unless you were being provocative and flirtatious).
- If their behaviour makes you in anyway uncomfortable, ask a leader of the opposite sex whom the young individual trusts to talk with him or her, letting them know you are not interested.
- If things become very difficult and intense then, with another leader, confront the young person. Let them know your complete lack of interest and how the situation makes you feel. Reassure them you will put the situation out of your mind and won't speak of it again.

PROBLEM
I'm not sure I'm cut out for this!

Category   *Called or chosen?*

Symptoms   *Dislike of young people.*
Hate going to youth group.
Resent being asked to do youth work by the geeky church minister.
Will pay anyone to take my place?

Case History

It was a Sunday afternoon fellowship group, and I had only been the youth pastor two weeks. I was still in my observing and 'learning on my feet' mode. Peter, one of the existing leaders of the fellowship group, was taking the Bible study. I had not had much chance to meet and talk with my leaders, so my only impression of him was from his general appearance. He was in his mid-forties, heavily built and seemed a fairly firm sort of bloke.

With his opening words of: 'Sit down and shut up!' he had my attention. 'If anyone talks while I'm leading this afternoon, you will be banned for a month'. Sure enough he kept his word – there were three people banned that afternoon. One person was dragged out of his seat and shoved across the other side of the room, because Peter had caught him smiling at the person next to him. Another one was made to stand facing the corner because he had accidentally broken wind.

Peter's subject that afternoon was the grace of God. Though his theology was faultless, his youth work skills and his actions were highly questionable. Peter stopped the group on two occasions to shout at the thirty or so terrified young people who, in my opinion, were being as good as gold. With twenty minutes to go, he stopped the meeting for a final time, muttered to himself, lifted his head and informed everybody they were so awful he didn't even know why he bothered! Turning round, he picked up his Bible and left the room.

I found myself asking the very same question. Why did he bother? It certainly didn't look as if he was enjoying himself and even if he was, the youth group weren't! I caught up with Peter later that week to talk about what I had seen at the fellowship group. He was quick to inform me the only reason he did help out was because six months back, the Church minister had made a plea, asking for people to help out in the youth fellowship group. There and then, after only two weeks in my new position, I thanked my first youth leader for his help – and fired him.

Care Plans

Every church youth leader I know – myself included – has, at some point, asked themselves why they carry on. Whether it be youth clubs, fellowship groups, creative groups, outreach, social activities or school work, we have asked: 'Am I good at it, do I enjoy it and do I really want to invest all my time in it?' I'm sure at one time or other you have asked one or all of these questions.

With increasing pressure from local churches who are putting youth work high on their agendas, both willing and unwilling people are pushed into making commitments to work with young people. There is a desire to be relevant and meet the needs of today's generation of teenagers. Jesus said: 'The harvest is plentiful, but the workers are few'. (Matt. 9:37) The reality today is the workers are increasing but in many situations the harvest is not plentiful. Young people are not storming the churches, considering the amount of resource invested in youth ministries.

So what's the reason? More often than not, it's because in the desperation to fill the need we are replacing quality with quantity. Many leaders, like Peter, have either volunteered or been volunteered to help in youth ministry out of a need rather than from a sense of calling. If you are wondering whether you have been called by God rather than merely chosen by a church, or whether you really are cut out for youth work, you may find it helpful to see if you identify with these three genuine reasons for taking up youth work:

A call from God

Be involved in youth work because you have been called by God and have a peace about your involvement. If you have a heart and love for young people, then the likelihood is you are responding to a call. You should not be involved in youth ministry because your name was put forward and selected by the church council or minister. Many helpers are good people who want to serve where the need is. I suggest if you are helping because of the need and youth work is something you don't particularly enjoy or feel directly called to, that you ask the minister to allow you to serve in areas to which you feel more guided and where you will be more at home.

If, however, you feel God may be calling you, but are not sure, simply pray about it. Ask others, whom you trust, to pray about it as well, and seek together to establish which area you should be involved in, whether that is a new one, or one where you are already serving. See how things develop from there. Maybe you are resisting God's voice. Jonah had no intentions of fulfilling his calling; he had no time for the people in Nineveh and the last place he wanted to be was in that God-forsaken city. It may well be that the last place you want to be is Sunday night youth group but if God has called you to it, then you will make a considerable difference to the lives of young people by being there.

A love for young people

Be involved in youth work because you love young people and enjoy being around them. To be a youth worker does not mean you have to speak the 'in' language, wear the 'in' clothes or listen to the 'in' music. Nor does it mean you have to be the best communicator when it comes to Bible studies. The reality is, the best youth leaders I know do none of these things. They simply love being with young people and young people love being with them. Young people are human beings; they can sense if you like them and enjoy being around them. It doesn't matter whether you're twenty-two or eighty-five. If you love them they will love you back. Many youth leaders enjoy being around young people but are shy and often don't know what to say, so they hold back altogether. If you're shy, here's a quick line for you: 'Don't give up!' Ask God to help you, pray for the young people and pray that you can find common ground to help you to talk and communicate more freely. I have met some people who love young people but are not called, yet I have never met anybody who feels he or she is called but dislikes young people. Love is part of the calling!

An appreciation of the need

Be a youth worker because you sense the need and importance of youth work. To be truly effective means both seeing the need and also the world the young person lives in. You don't need fully to understand the culture that surrounds them, but it does help to understand the pressures that arise in their lives, such as exams or a death in the family. Climb into their world, laugh with them and even cry with them.

Youth work does not come naturally to everyone but that doesn't mean you are not called. Leadership didn't come so naturally to Moses. He needed his brother-in-law to help him, yet it was Moses who was called first, not Aaron. Many good youth workers have developed skills and techniques over time and now have great ministries affecting dozens of teenagers. Our calling and our abilities may not go hand in hand. God doesn't need able people, just willing people who have responded to his voice.

Yet our love for young people should be apparent. In 1 Thessalonians 2:8 it says Paul didn't just love the church in Thessalonica: he had invested his life in them. As youth workers, we must invest our very lives in the people we work with and to whom we minister. It's a calling followed by a commitment, not to a meeting but to the lives of young people.

Action page

Questionnaire – Am I cut out for Youth work?

(tick next to appropriate sentence, and then circle the correct statement at the end of each point)

Am I called?
- I have prayed about it and feel I should be involved in youth work ☐
- Others whom I trust have prayed about it and feel I should be involved in youth work ☐
- I have never prayed about it but have been involved in youth work for some time now ☐
- I have been asked by the minister or church council because no one else is doing it ☐

I feel called to youth work – Yes/No

Do I love young people?
- I have a real love for young people and enjoy being with them ☐
- I have a love and a burden for young people ☐
- I wouldn't say I have a love for young people but do have a burden ☐
- I don't enjoy being with young people but am involved with them for other reasons ☐

I feel it is right that I am working with young people – Yes/No

Do I understand young people?
- I have always felt able to relate well to young people and understand what they are facing ☐
- I understand some of the pressures they may be facing but struggle to relate to it ☐
- I have no idea what is going on in their heads but love being with them ☐

- I have no idea what's going on in their heads and don't enjoy being with them   ☐

I feel I am in the right area of ministry at this time – Yes/No

If you can answer 'yes' to all three questions then youth work is most likely for you. If you have one 'no' answer, then perhaps you should be carefully considering whether you are currently in the most appropriate ministry.

PROBLEM
What do I do with the leaders I have?

Category *Leading a team*

Symptoms *The new leaders never do anything but sit in the corner, looking stressed.*
Your assistant leader has split away, taking half the group with him.
All the leaders have gone on strike demanding more involvement.

Case History

Tom had arranged a meeting about the coming youth camp, with the three other leaders who would be attending. He started the meeting by producing a copy of the timetable, fully laid out with clear instructions about what was happening. He told them 'As you can see I have done the programme. There are just a couple of blanks next to items where I need to put your names, so have a look and decide what you want to do'.

The three leaders began to absorb the programme and after a moment Jenny responded: 'Tom, the only things available are the cooking, cleaning and bedtime duties'. Her tone was one of protest. 'Is that a problem?' Tom asked. Bill chipped in 'It's just a bit odd really, Tom, you seem to be leading all the talks, the wild games, the walk, the outdoor adventure games and the entertainment night.' Tom looked bemused: whatever the point was he was missing it. 'Can't you see I will be working very hard on the camp? All I'm asking for is a bit of help from you on these minor duties. After all, I was hoping you had come to serve.' The remark cut deep. Jenny sat upright and looked intensely at Tom.

'Of course we are here to serve, but we expect you to as well. You are working too hard, but not in a servant capacity – you are being very selfish. You are doing all the pleasurable things, while we are confined to cleaning, cooking or shouting at people to go to bed!'

Care plans

It seems strange that many of us are continually crying out for new leaders, yet when we get them we never really know what to do with them. So many team leaders could give a list of things with which they need help. Yet when team members arrive, they often find themselves in the corner, wondering what to do, or being asked to do those tasks no one else wants to take on. If you are a good youth worker then being around young people is all you want to do. You take every opportunity to be with them, enjoying their company. Many good youth leaders are poor team leaders, not because they have no leadership qualities or administrative abilities but because they cannot share the relationship and input they have with the young people.

What makes a good team leader?
- A good team leader uses his or her team to its maximum capacity. Many church youth leaders turn up for the events. Perhaps they have a conversation with the young people, they sit through the meeting, have another conversation at the end of the meeting and then go home. That's great if that is all they are supposed to be doing. But often the reality is that the gifting and potential of each of our leaders is being underused by as much as ninety per cent. More often than not, the fault lies with the main youth worker. I have been in this situation on many occasions – despite having six or seven good youth leaders around me, I continually struggle to give up the best parts of the work. I find all sorts of reasons, such as I'm not convinced anyone could do the job better, which probably means I would hate anyone to do the job better.

  Like Tom, it's easier to take all the cream and leave the drudgery for others. We need to learn how to pool our resources, not allowing our greatest assets, the other leaders, to go flabby and redundant in the corner.

- A good team leader is able to evaluate the gifting or potential gifting of current leaders. They have a willingness to delegate jobs according to strengths, even if it means someone takes their favourite jobs.
- A good team leader holds a vision that unites their team around them – all thinking alike and all rooting for the same thing. Take a moment to think: 'Does everyone in my team know what the youth work in the church or centre is doing, why it does it and where the youth work is going?' Ask your leaders separately – if they are unsure then it is your role to help them to see your vision and to excite them with it.
- A good team leader leads by example rather than being excessively authoritarian. A leader who serves with humility, kindness and fairness will be served with loyalty and favour by their staff. You should be willing to give up speaking opportunities or leading games in order to swap roles with another leader and clean the kitchen or make the drinks.
- A good leader accepts criticism and is willing to change their position on issues and directions. If we show we are listening and are responsive to suggestions, then we learn ideas and the others feel valued. Involving others in planning and direction will allow them to feel a part of the process, as well as gaining their support in achieving whatever we are planning to do.

When selecting members for your team then make sure firstly that you choose those who love young people, and secondly that you choose those who will fit the particular jobs you have. Take a moment to think through the kind of leadership positions there are, and what is currently required in your group. Here is a list of possible jobs

- Relational worker/group leader
- Communicator/Bible Study leader/preacher
- Group work co-ordinator
- Worship leader/musician

- Games leader
- Driver
- General helper – cook/assistant etc
- Trainee leaders
- Programme co-ordinator
- Tidy upper
- Prayer co-ordinator

How many of those roles are you personally taking on each week? How many of the above are taken on by your existing leaders? How can more responsibility be distributed among new and existing leaders? Do you have any leaders whose gifts are not being used in the appropriate areas?

Delegation is the mark of a good leader – but so is wisdom. Don't give leaders roles that they have no gifting for, nor any likelihood of developing those gifts. But for many, with time and guidance, new roles and skills can be learnt. Take time with each of your leaders, going through each area available to see where their gifts lie. Our aim should be to raise staff into positions of leadership, where they will be able to continue the programme with or without us. Not leaders who just watch and feel helpless when we are absent.

In Matthew 20:25–27 Jesus says 'Whoever wants to be great among you must be a servant'. A leader should not see their role as wielding power over others and taking all the glory. Instead, they must use the leaders God has given them, and lead them into higher positions of responsibility. The aim is to have assistant leaders who are giving one hundred per cent of their gifts, and a youth ministry which is reaping the reward of your successful leadership.

Action Page

Evaluate your leadership

- What three things do you most enjoy doing in youth work?

- What three things do you least enjoy doing?

- What three jobs do you reckon as just 'OK'?

- What one thing do you do that no one else can do as well as you?

- What new or existing leaders can do the things you hate doing?

- Do they do them because you told them to or because they enjoy them and are good at them?

- What new or existing leaders do the things you most enjoy doing?

- Do they do them because you asked them to or because they are good at them?

- Does anyone do the one thing that you are good at?

- How do you think other leaders view your leadership style?

After reflecting on the above questions, what do you think needs to change in your leadership? What have they confirmed that you are doing right in your leadership?

PROBLEM
Is fifteen too young to be a youth leader?

Category   *Youth leadership*

Symptoms   *Chaos!*
Beer, cigarettes. and needles are passed around with the Bibles.
Leaders who can shave and are over 16 are not permitted to attend.

Case History

Lorna had been nothing but trouble as a twelve-year-old in my youth group. Complaining was what she did best. I can well remember the meetings when I would come away, deeply discouraged because she had wrecked the venue and disrupted the atmosphere. I would have been forced to abandon the meeting. Nothing ever seemed quite right for her, and secretly I would have been happy if she had left the group. Yet if she had, I would have lost one of my best leaders ever to come out of a group. With perseverance and commitment, Lorna became a clear and gifted group leader. So much so she became my assistant leader at just fifteen. Now in her early twenties, Lorna is pioneering a church in the heart of the Midlands.

It's an amazing thing when a member of your youth group, especially a problem one, goes on to mature and serve God in exciting ways. You realise what a miracle God has done and are glad that somewhere along the way, you had something to do with it.

Care Plans

Every youth worker's cry is for more leaders. Often some leaders look after twenty or thirty young people without help. Young people need older role models and youth leaders need the experience of mature Christians standing beside them. So it is critical that we draw members of our congregations into youth leadership. Yet it is equally critical that we look for and nurture leadership skills in the younger members of our youth groups. Each group has its emerging talented leaders who need adults to draw alongside, encourage, develop and equip them into future positions. The best football teams in our country are those who take youth training schemes seriously. Spotting the talent young and investing hours of skill and experience always pays back later for the club. It's no different for us in youth work; most of my working week has always been involved in drawing alongside young leaders and giving them everything I have to offer. In fact I've often been criticised for wasting time on certain people. Wherever I've gone and whatever I've done, I've always tried to hand as much of the leadership and responsibility over to younger people as possible, for two real reasons

* So that the young person grows with the invested responsibility. No one wants to fail someone who has given them a position of importance. On the contrary, they want to prove they are worthy of such a position. Because of that, and as long as they remain humble, they will learn and grow in their skills and experience.
* So that the young person and group (if in a group environment) feel a sense of ownership. The control of what is happening no longer revolves around an older leadership, who often seem to dictate the way things go. It gives a new feel when the group has some say and direction. Naturally a good youth leader will allow the group always to feel this way, while subtly and yet firmly being in control of the direction and events that take place.

For some, a third reason would be to give numerical support when there are no adult leaders around to help. Naturally, young people can offer themselves and can fill the particular need. Yet you must make sure you do not overburden them nor give them responsibility that they cannot fulfil, either because of their immaturity, or for legal reasons (e.g. guardianship over younger members on a weekend away). Nor should you use younger leaders for this purpose only, but see it as a commitment to them in their development. We must also be sensitive towards the young person's outside interests, social life and also to school pressures such as exams and homework.

We should be careful, therefore, not to place too much responsibility on them when demands from elsewhere put them in the position of having to decide what is more important. Instead, we should encourage them to give their attention to other pressing issues, showing them that as the leader you are giving them both freedom and your trust. This course of action will always bring support from their home. Many youth leaders know how it feels to have a phone call from a parent, because their child has not studied for an exam because they were at church or involved in youth department-related issues.

What areas of leadership can I help a young person develop in?

Often a young person's first exposure to leadership is when they are asked to lead a discussion group or some form of group work. As long as the group does not have psychotic tendencies and the young person has sufficient verbal skills and confidence, then it should be a positive experience. Have a leader nearby to help out if things start to go wrong. Occasionally group dynamics (too many shy people or too many loud people, or lack of clear instructions) can make leading a group pretty unpleasant. An older hand nearby to smooth out any difficulties will give reassurance – without being seen as interfering, patronising or undermining the young person's developing authority.

As they grow, try to involve the young leader in other areas such as ice-breakers, giving out the notices, leading the prayer time, leading the worship (if they're musically gifted) and, when they are really coming on, leading the evening meeting and teaching.

Problems with young leaders

You are guaranteed to face problems with young leaders. The three main areas I have commonly encountered are their lack of experience, their lack of maturity and a lack of maturity from the group.

Lack of experience

The young leader should be expected to make mistakes. Common ones are dominating discussions, continually giving their opinion, coming down hard on members of the group, not controlling the group, not understanding what they are really doing, and being out of their depth in understanding the discussion. Gentle guidance, with positive direction and praise for what they did correctly, should help overcome such difficulties. Whenever possible, have a time for feedback, for the young leader and the main leader. This provides an opportunity for both to learn and increases their confidence. Always encourage!

Lack of maturity

Because they are still developing and very much adolescents themselves, you cannot expect things to go smoothly. Often the responsibility goes to their heads and is exchanged for the wrong type of authority: 'Do this because . . .' 'I'm leading tonight, so we do it this way . . .' 'Shut up, I'm in charge!'

Other areas where we can expect problems are with hormonal overdrives and just being cool in front of the opposite sex. These can have interesting consequences, if they use their authority to charm, flirt or just play the fool. Some leaders have much talent but some questionable attitudes, either because of hang-ups or adolescent needs. You will need to pray each week for their difficulties to be overcome. Each of these problems need to be tackled with the young leader to help them to see that to maintain a position of responsibility then they must act responsibly.

Lack of maturity from the group

Occasionally, if the group is particularly immature, both spiritually and emotionally, they may be unwilling to respect a chosen peer as a small group leader, or to take them seriously when they lead Bible studies. Observe carefully why the group struggle with the leader. It could be the timing is just not yet right.

Every young person in one way or another comes with the baggage of adolescence. For some their bags are bigger and others carry additional bags with problems that need serious attention. We need to be wise in whom we choose but responsibility has the amazing habit of helping young people lose their rubbish. Their self-image improves and, with confidence, their personality develops and new abilities emerge.

The parable of the talents (Mt. 25:14–30) can be taken to imply that God has invested us as youth leaders with talented young people. If we do not use their talents or help them develop, then we are as guilty as the man who simply buried his talent. Let us raise up leaders in our groups who will go on into adulthood and help advance the Kingdom in ways we only ever dream about!

Action Page

How would I develop a young leader?

- Spot their talent and willingness to learn.
- Find areas to introduce them gently to leading that will give them a positive experience.
- Draw alongside them, with encouragement, giving positive feed-back and guidelines.
- As they develop gently remove your own presence. Allow them to feel fully responsible and to grow in their own style, not one imposed by overly cautious leaders. Do not give unconditional responsibility or be too far from the scene. Just don't appear to be around eavesdropping, or adding unnecessary advice to the young leader, as this undermines them, and highlights your own insecurities.
- Allow mistakes: failure in a controlled environment should be accepted as it makes for growth. We all learn from our mistakes.
- As young leaders become more confident, they can be given new areas of responsibility with new challenges, allowing more depth to their development and growth.
- Actively encourage feedback from the young leader, let them voice their successes, failures and fears.
- Heap praise upon praise on a young leader. Remember one negative remark holds as much weight as ten positive ones. Don't be afraid to criticise, but make sure it's constructive and that there are plenty of positive comments before and after it.

PROBLEM
Do parents go to hell?

Category   *Living with hot potatoes*

Symptoms   *The local newspaper has your name on front page in big bold letters saying 'Youth worker condemns non-churchgoers, homosexuals, divorcees, fat people, nose pickers and generally life itself'.*

Case History

Jo had been asked to lead the Bible study on judgement. She was asked because her knowledge of the Bible was far greater than any of the other leaders, and she also happened to be fairly gentle in her approach. After only ten minutes into the study, the fifteen or so young people began to make noises among themselves. Jo, aware something was going on, continued the study until Carl, a fourteen-year-old who was usually the quietest member of the group, stopped her in her tracks. He asked her if she was really saying those who didn't know Jesus and trusted in him, would not go to heaven. Jo's response was slow and thoughtful: 'Well Carl, it's hard for us to take it in but the Bible is very clear that everyone is sinful and we need to be clean from sin to enter heaven'.

Carl sat quietly for a moment, then replied: 'Are you saying that Christians are the only ones who can be made clean?' Jo knew this was more than a general question. 'What I'm saying is that only those who have asked Jesus for forgiveness and given their lives to him are made clean'. Carl didn't hesitate in his next question: 'Jo, my dad is a Christian but my mum never comes to church and tells my dad she doesn't believe in God. Does that mean she is going to hell?' Somewhat trapped by the question, with every young person's eyes upon her, she looked to the other leaders for inspiration and help. None was given. Her reply was slow and chilling: 'You need to come to your own conclusion; I'm just telling you what the Bible says and what I believe to be true'. Carl muttered loud enough for all to hear 'You're saying she's going to hell!'

Care Plans

Some would say the truth is the truth and therefore the truth must be told. There are many hot potatoes that the best and most articulate of leaders would prefer to avoid. Yet if we are going to teach the morals and theological truths that we hold on to, we must expect young people to take our message personally. Sometimes they will even be offended by it. If the young people aren't offended, their parents may well be. Subjects like divorce, sex outside marriage, masturbation, homosexuality and issues of salvation may well provoke hostile responses. We are living and working with people in the real world; for most it's a broken world with very few absolutes. The church can be seen as pious and hypocritical, lording its highly moralistic views over the community.

Yet the reality is Jesus lived and mixed in such a world showing compassion and love, not heaping guilt and rules but freedom and liberation. What do we say about the absolutes of love and sexuality, when members of our group have divorced parents now living with partners they are not married to? When one parent is caught up in an extra-marital affair? When someone is being raised by their parent who is gay and who lives with a gay partner? What do we say about salvation when many of our teenagers' parents are not believers? Like Jo, many leaders have been attacked by members of their group for daring to even vaguely suggest a parent may not be going to heaven. Some leaders have had parents phone them up, asking if they really said they were going to hell. The answer of course was 'yes' and 'no'. No, the leader didn't say that particular parent was going to hell. Yes, they did say unless a person knows and has faith in Jesus, they will not be going to heaven. We may try and deal with issues as diplomatically and softly as we know how, but the listener may either misunderstand what was said or take it to heart, blatantly disagreeing.

When dealing with issues that could offend, it is important that we know our audience. For example, if we say the rules on love and sex are to have one partner for life, think first about those in your group who have divorced parents. How will they respond; when did their parents split and what affect did it have? On issues such as salvation think through which members of the group have not made a commitment and which members of the group have non-Christian parents. With the issue of homosexuality, how many young people do you have in your group who are struggling with their own sexual identity, unsure of how they feel? The likelihood is that you will not know, but a good proportion of the boys in your group will, at one time or other, have had confused thoughts and feelings. With the information we have, we must make a decision on how sensitive we will be and how best to tackle the issues at hand. At times we can be so diplomatic that actually no one hears the main point, because it came in so much wrapping paper. We may want to talk with some people first, asking them if such a subject is something they want to be around for. Can they deal with it, or is it just too painful? With others, we may well need to give reassurance and support afterwards. In controversial issues, being clear, gentle and non-judgmental is so very important. Being firmly in control of where things are going is also important.

Allowing people to have their say should always be encouraged, but diplomacy and sensitivity need to be emphasised. I'm sure you have been there when one young person pours a heap of guilt on someone else in the group, or when one teenager reveals far more about themselves, in the heat of the moment than they would later have wished. If at all applicable, when dealing with a sensitive issue such as divorce, call on leaders or mature members of the group who have faced difficult situations. Ask them to describe what it felt like and what it did to their family life, having to work through hard times, such as having a parent leave home.

Alongside individual testimony and first-hand accounts, it is important for us not to encroach on subjects that we have little knowledge about. The more provocative a subject is the more we should give our time and energy to researching the details and holding a balanced viewpoint. If as leaders we are unsure what we believe, the meeting may well end in sheer confusion. (Rom. 14:5b) We should allow room for individual differences of opinion, as long as we know our own minds and the direction the meeting is heading.

As youth leaders it is our role to love and protect those who come to us for leadership advice and direction. We should offer encouragement and affirmation to the many who bear the scars of the real world, never pointing our fingers or heaping condemnation on the teenager or his family. That is not for us to do (Lk. 6:37). In every circumstance let us speak with wisdom, using our words to bring healing (Prov. 12:18). In every group we will have people who disagree and hold different views from our own. We should avoid arguments and debates over issues that are merely provocative or not important as these can be unhelpful, as well as being contrary to scripture. (Rom. 14:1–3)

We are here to tell the truth, speak the truth and live the truth. Naturally the truth we know is a truth of absolutes, and though Jesus showed real compassion to the sinners he mingled with, he told the truth, never compromising the ways of God. Jesus urged the people to walk in the ways of God, pointing out that their own ways were misguided and had eternal consequences. So we should encourage those we work with to do the same. Freedom and liberation are found in the truth, for Jesus said the 'truth will set you free'. (Jn. 8:32). However, we must never move from the fact that the way of the Gospel is costly, and that cost is that we are to be different from the rest of the world (Mt. 5:10, 7:13,14). The Bible is offensive to those who do not hold its values. We will never escape offending some people, but we should not deliberately offend and our aim must be to follow, with the Spirit's help, Christ's example of sensitivity, compassion and love.

Action Page
When leading a debate on controversial issues

- Avoid making it personal.
- Be sensitive and discreet.
- Know your audience.
- Talk with those who may find the discussion too painful or personal beforehand.
- Offer reassurance and affirmation afterwards to those bruised in any way from the meeting.
- Be clear, gentle and non-judgmental.
- Be firmly in control of the group and the direction of the meeting.
- Prevent wild and offensive comments from the floor.
- Try to prevent revealing and personal comments people may later regret.
- Do not condemn.
- Do not compromise what you hold to be true for the sake of avoiding hostility. Instead, stop the meeting and resume another time when people may be more able to deal with the issue.
- Be loving.

PROBLEM
Am I really expected to take on the family as well as the young person?

Category   *Parents*

Symptoms   *Without the formalities, you have become the full-time guardian of twenty young people as twenty sets of parents pass on their responsibilities to you. As mediator between teenager and parent, you earn two black eyes each meeting. One from each teenager.*

Case History

Jane put the phone down, wondering what the conversation had been about. John's father had phoned her, the full-time youth worker of a prosperous Anglican church. He had been so irate that she was struggling to understand the points he had made. That evening Jane had told John he was just too young for the confirmation classes that were to start that month. His father was obviously unhappy with the decision. The only thing Jane did understand from the phone call was the ultimatum: either she prepared his son for confirmation or they'd find another church who would.

The following Sunday Jane received some very long and hard stares from members of the congregation. With courage she asked why she was receiving such looks. The reply from someone she regarded as a friend was: 'I think it is awful, you telling someone they should leave the church and have their son confirmed elsewhere. I mean who are you to say such things?'

Knowing she had never made such a remark and yet also realising the whole church believed she had, Jane caved in. She allowed John to join the confirmation class. The following day she received a card, saying how much the family appreciated her ministry in the church. It was signed by John's father.

Care Plans

What is it that can drive a youth worker mad with anger, paranoid with fear or ecstatic with joy? The answer is parents. If we have been around for long in youth work, then the likelihood is we will have an accumulation of scars from heated meetings with unhappy parents. We remember the confrontations and the hurtful remarks more than we remember the encouragements, affirmations and demonstrations of support. It is certainly true that most parents are genuinely delighted in what we do, pleased that someone is actually interested in their child, willing to spend time with them, take them off their hands and have good input into their son's or daughter's life. We often miss the mum or dad that hangs about that little bit longer after an event when collecting their son or daughter, or the smile as they leave, the hand shake and the remark: 'Thanks'. Usually it's because we are so wrapped up in getting rid of everyone and tidying the building. Yet if we just stopped and spent a moment with each parent, we would leave feeling the appreciation they want to express.

Being a youth worker is a stressful job in itself, but being a full-time parent with one or more adolescents is something to be admired. Most parents actually have no idea what they are doing when it comes to leading their children through adolescence; they are surviving at best. What with mood swings, hygiene issues, phone bills, discipline problems, clothing expenses, other parents' teenagers and school reports, packing them off to the church youth group is a delight, or at least a relief. We should try and see these guardians as heroes who are often over-stressed busy people with families to keep on the straight and narrow. The reality is we must make every opportunity to be their allies and their support. Youth work is a partnership between you, the young person and the parents.

When a parent comes thumping at our door, or shouts down the telephone, rather than becoming defensive and deciding this is one fight we are going to win, take a moment to hear the points being made – are they valid? Often they do not merit the aggression we are being hit over the head with. The fact is when we take on a young person in our groups, we take on the family and with that family comes family stress and personalities. Being reprimanded for allowing someone's son to come to the youth group when he was under a curfew (which you didn't know about) or for the fact someone's daughter didn't come straight home after leaving your meeting, is hardly your fault. Yet parents need support, they are often beside themselves with frustration over a disobedient rebellious teen. Dumping a load on you is hardly fair, but it is a partnership.

Into such a partnership there may come unfair expectations such as: 'I can't get through to him – I expect you to!' When we do not achieve this, there may well be no acknowledgement for our trying but quite likely criticism for failing. It is not unknown for parents to abuse such open relationships by making youth workers scapegoats for their own inadequacies. We find ourselves continually at the centre of a problem with their child. Issues that are just not there or are very minor become such huge headaches that the entire Christian community comes to hear about it. It's really a case of 'take the log out of your own eye before removing the speck from the youth worker's eye', but we just can't say that to a bruised parent and usually we end up taking it straight on the chin.

Jesus didn't come 'to be served but to serve' (Mt. 20:28) and in our roles as youth leaders we should mirror this. In serving we can expect hassles, complications and dirt. It is our job to help young people with their adolescent needs as well as their spiritual needs. Yet it is the parents who have been given the full-time role of raising their children in the training and instructions of the Lord (Eph. 6:4). We do not carry the responsibility for their development – thankfully that is in the hands of their parents or guardians, whether Christians or not. Therefore we are a support facility for those who have been given that responsibility.

Working with parents, who are usually full of encouragement but can be disgruntled at times, is part of our job descriptions. The youth worker can be a real help with the parents' burdens. Not only by taking time every week to invest the things of God into the lives of their children, but also by being courteous and working through those adolescent issues with the teenager that the family is struggling with. An open line, an open door and being available to parents will lead to a successful partnership.

Action Page

How to have a successful partnership with parents

- Always remember the parent is the one who raises the teenager, day in day out.
- Always abide by the rules of the parents. e.g., on the weekend away: 'Bed by 11 p.m. at the latest'. However, rules must be reasonable and not conflict with every other parents' expectations
- Actively keep an open door and be approachable to parents.
- Listen to criticism and ask for time before responding to the complaint – be humble rather than proud. Humility speaks volumes. However, it may be appropriate to reflect unreasonable comments that are either personal or 'off the wall', back to the person who made them to expose their irrational nature.
- Tell parents when their expectations of you are unrealistic.
- Inform parents of your intentions when dealing with their child e.g. 'I will talk with your son about it. The conversation will remain between the two of us, unless I feel it is so serious that you need to know. Are you happy with that?'
- Keep parents in touch with what you are doing and planning.
- Send home annual reports of what has happened over the year in the youth work.
- Arrange a parents' forum once or twice a year where parents can come and express their concerns or praise. Great training events can emerge from forums.
- Make a point of visiting or talking on the phone with parents every six months or so.
- Be diplomatic, but never be afraid to tell parents when their child has overstepped the mark or done something so wrong it can't be overlooked.
- Be prepared for a parent to disagree when (and if) you have to inform them their child is not behaving.

PROBLEM
How do I deal with pranks?

Category   *Mischievous disorder.*

Symptoms   *Unbelievable hatred towards a young person.*
General fear for your life.
Increased prayer life asking God for a call to minister to the geriatric.

Case History

It was my last weekend away with my youth group and it also happened to be the last time I would be with them before I moved abroad. I knew some kind of prank was in order so I slept with my bag, wallet and car keys inside my sleeping bag. Beside my pillow I had a baseball bat just as a warning for any lurking intruders. I had taken the bed furthest away from anyone else. Each of the nights had gone peacefully but I awoke on the last morning to screams of laughter. Jumping out of my bed I ran for the window and found that my two year-old car, for which I had just found a buyer, had been covered in graffiti. Inside the vehicle were dozens of Santa Clauses and hundreds of balloons. That did not concern me, but what did was the fact that the car keys were still in my sleeping bag and I had made sure each of the car doors was locked the night before. It turned out the joker had used some highly illegal car breaking equipment to force the door open at 4 in the morning. To try and clean the car before the graffiti became too permanent, I rushed to the toilet to grab a bucket of water. Before I knew it the toilet door swung closed and was jammed on the other side by an upside down broom handle. I was trapped. No amount of bargaining would release me and I had to force my way out. The door broke in the struggle, and on clambering past the hanging door dozens of eggs flew across the room, followed by milk, sugar and flour – all with precise targeting. Now I know that in some strange way these were acts of affection but the damage caused to the car, the building, and my stained clothes made me want to chop up each of the culprits with an axe.

Care plans

My own painful experiences of pranks are just the tip of a large iceberg. Friends and colleagues of mine have endured such practical jokes as nearly being drowned in swimming pools, food poisoning, and being tied to a pole and stripped down by members of the youth group. Why are these pranks not funny? Because you as the youth leader have lost control and there is nothing you can do other than use brute force to regain control. When you need to use force then you have stepped outside the ethic of a safe youth ministry.

Pranks are fun, or at least meant to be. Yet when they cause damage, become indecent or threaten your health then a line must be drawn. How can we draw the line without becoming the world's biggest kill-joy? The answer is so simple we often over-look it

- Make it clear at the start of all events that a firm line is drawn between what is acceptable and what is not. Give your group space to have their own creative fun. Don't come down so heavy that they feel restricted to the point of no enjoyment.
- Make it clear that anything that even vaguely goes over that line will not be acceptable and will result in some form of disciplining. Explain what that discipline will be. Make sure you act on what you say!
- Offer a much more exciting alternative. Let them have plenty of fun so they don't need to create their own destructive pranks. At events like weekends away, fill the programme to exhaustion, then any free time they do have will be used more sociably.
- Having a good proportion of leaders helps to keep things under control, not just for monitoring, but because the more leaders

you have the more energy can be poured into the group. In the case of pranks after or before events, make sure sufficient leaders are around to watch out for any possible trouble (like unwanted flour bombs).

In 2 Thessalonians 3:14,15, Paul instructs the church that those who did not keep to the rules laid down by Paul in following Jesus should be disciplined. As leaders it is fair for us to make similar decisions if our rules are ignored. Perhaps we may not want to exclude the guilty from the group but some form of non-physical discipline should be used.

Through humiliating and some times painful experiences, I learned that the desire to be a trendy and fun youth leader may be at the expense of one's programme, integrity, possibly one's health and that of others. Have fun by all means, in fact have amazing fun, but as the leader you should be in control of what is happening around you.

Action page

Suggested Guidelines for pranks and general conduct

- Have fun.
- Your fun must not be at the cost of someone else's happiness or cause humiliation.
- Your fun must not involve damage to anyone's property (including your own).
- Your fun must not physically hurt anybody.
- Your fun must not inflict on anybody something they do not desire.
- Your fun must not damage the building.
- Your fun must not be an inconvenience to others.
- Your fun must be legal.
- Your fun must not conflict with the programme.
- Your fun should be enjoyed by others as well as yourself.

COMPLAINT
He only broke his arm!

Category   *Games that don't kill*

Symptoms   *Want to die inside.*
May want to retire there and then.
An inevitable meeting with the parent from hell is moments away.

Case History

The games evening had become a success within the community. Dave didn't normally get any help from other church leaders but this week was an exception. The kids came because they loved the creativity and the wildness of each evening. However, this evening was to be more wild than he had expected. The leader who had come to help insisted in joining in on one of the games, which happened to be a unique style of basket ball. In the excitement of the moment he tackled one of the thirteen-year-old boys, breaking his arm. Having to deal with the injured boy, Dave foolishly left the leader in charge while contacting the boy's parents to take him on to casualty. He returned to find someone else had dislocated their fingers, and one of the girls had gone home with a throbbing headache and a suspected broken nose. The news leaked out to many of the parents and attendance at the games evenings, which had attracted many non-churchgoing kids, took a drastic dip.

Care Plans

Games evenings and games in general are to be encouraged in your programmes. Often they are the highlight of meetings and of weekends away. They help form great relationships, knock down any uncomfortable tensions, get rid of too much energy which you just don't want in your Bible study and can be excellent fun and value. Yet to my regret I have painfully experienced many casualties, including broken bones, concussion and severe vomiting. Most common of all are the torn or stained clothes, which for a young person are a major problem (as they are nearly always designer labelled). Youth leaders hate grumpy parents even more than a grumpy teenager and, as I'm sure you will have experienced, they can come pretty grumpy and at times ugly.

It is therefore important that when we put those excellent wacky games into our programme we do not risk subjecting ourselves to the dreaded interview with a resentful parent. Or even worse – a trip to casualty with a highly strung teenager, who tells everyone who asks him what happened that it was all your fault.

When you have your games make the following decisions:-

- I want it to be fun.
- I want it to be safe.
- I want it to have only positive repercussions.

So how can I achieve these three points?

- Make sure the person who is leading the games remains firmly in control. In all the excitement other leaders or young people like a piece of the action but their contribution may not be to the standards you have set.
- Make sure you have a good ratio of leaders to spot and defuse potential problems
- Ensure that your leaders do not involve themselves in semi-aggressive games like wild games. If they do then they should have a non-contact role.
- Is the game suitable for the environment? Very physical games may not work in living rooms.
- Explain the rules carefully and point out that if the rules are ignored the offending player may be excluded.
- Do you have the appropriate equipment for the game? Wrong material can result in injuries.

- Use common sense. Often potential problems are obvious. Should Gary who is six foot two inches, and weighs seventeen stone, be tackling Louise who is only five foot two and weighs eight stone?
- Put a time scale on all your activities. Many injuries happen after the game has finished through confusion as to whether it is still being played.
- Night games are fantastic but make sure, if you're not using torches, that all the players are familiar with the landscape. I've had people fall in ditches, trip over tree stumps and get lost in woods.
- Be in control at all times. Be able to make contact and be heard by all whenever you need to. Use either a whistle, a megaphone or a microphone. There is nothing worse than seeing a problem and not being able to stop it.

The crazier the games, the more attractive and dynamic your meetings will be. Have as many weird and wonderful games as your programme will allow. They bring an edge to your meetings that those straight-talking non-interactive groups could never hope to offer. You are bound to have your casualties but it's how many, how often and how serious they are that matters. Try and apply the above list to your programme and also have someone qualified in first aid in your group. Someone who knows what they are doing when things don't go smoothly can not only help the injured party but take the sting out of the criticisms you are bound to face. Ensure that the first aider is in touch with the current legal requirements set out for first aid. The law can change frequently on what help can or can't be administrated to minors.

Avoid those broken bones and agonising parent meetings by being safe. Don't substitute safety for fun. However don't substitute fun for boredom out of the paranoid fear that something may go wrong. Have plenty of wild and crazy controlled fun!

PROBLEM
'Is it all right to use force on someone causing problems?'

Category   *Youth conflict*

Symptom   *The radiator has been pulled off the wall and is coming at you.*
Your car has had all its wheels removed.
Someone has taken a liking to reshaping your nose.

Case History

It was the Sunday night late youth service. As ever, it was completely packed with young people from all across the district, everyone crammed into the gothic Anglican church. The windows were blacked out, special lighting effects were placed all around the building, the front of the church was leaking wires from every possible outlet. The PA system was so loud it could raise the dead buried under the church. The atmosphere was expectant. It should have been a good night.

Less than ten minutes after the service had started, about twelve lads who happened to be passing by and heard the noise wandered into the building. They sat and listened for a while and when a busty blonde got up to give her testimony, all hell broke lose. The group of lads started to whistle, chant and make all sorts of provocative remarks unsuitable for the evening. Mark, a volunteer helper for the service, who was only eighteen, raced out of his seat and ran for the group. 'Shut up, now!' he shouted. There was no response other than a few curses. The obscenities continued. Mark, who was a good deal taller than any of them, threatened that if they didn't pipe down he would throw them out. This only encouraged them to shout all the louder. Somewhat taken aback by the incident and fully aware that their chanting was ruining the evening, Mark panicked and kicked the guy with the biggest mouth. He swept the loudmouth's legs from under him and the guy crumpled up on the floor. Immediately they quietened down. Mark, who was now growing in confidence, told them as long as they were quiet they could stay. Afterwards all the leaders wanted to know what he had done to calm those yobs down. 'I just kicked one of them!' he replied.

Care Plans

When unwanted guests turn up doing unacceptable things or when even wanted guests lose it during meetings, dealing with the situation successfully is so important. We may all have felt like Mark in the past, just wanting to whack the perpetrator, though something tells us it's not a good move. Well, that's right; it's not a good move on three accounts:

- It's not ethical.
- It's not legal.
- It's not a positive solution.

It's easy for us to panic when a fight breaks out in the drop-in centre, or someone shouts and protests the whole way through a preach. Yet our response is critical; handled correctly the whole thing will die down and go away but handled badly then you may end up closing the club early and calling the police.

In my training days I was involved in a drop-in club where one evening two boys entered the building and started a fight with another boy. The whole thing wasn't dealt with properly and an entire riot broke out. We literally had to throw every young person out of the building and hold out inside with the doors locked until the police arrived. From outside they threw whatever they could at the windows and damaged the volunteers' cars in the car park. It was an experience I would not wish to be faced with again.

So how do we get it right without aggravating the situation or compromising our own standards and having to manhandle a young person?

Never panic. You will be forced to act in a way which may not be rational and which you may later regret. Instead, be very confident in your actions, appear to be in control and use positive body language. When dealing with the culprit show them respect – don't physically or verbally toss them aside as if they were rubbish but let them feel valued all the time. Don't humiliate them in any way. It is so easy for us to belittle young people; it can be a cheap form of power and can usually get us a laugh. The damage caused to a young person will last long after the laughter finishes, so always avoid humiliation techniques.

If your actions are gentle, controlled and respectful then the situation should resolve itself. These principles can be applied from the pulpit with a heckler to an outright vandal damaging your property.

Our ultimate guideline on what to do can be found in Matthew 5:43–48. Love your enemies and pray for them. In praying for those who cause us most problems the situation will change, even if the only change is in our attitude on how to deal with things. However that doesn't help when someone is about to bust a chair over your head. Jesus refers here to a practical love, a love shown by our actions. We may by all means protect ourselves and our volunteer leaders, but we must always avoid responding in a disrespectful and aggressive manner. Aggression does not work. Instead, heap love upon love onto the aggressor. In his ministry, Jesus had angry men with rocks ready to stone him, crowds trying to seize him (Jn. 10:31, 39) as well as continual verbal abuse, yet in every situation his response was positive, controlled and loving. It is essential that we learn to deal with conflict in a way that will not leave us embarrassed or regretful when the heat of the moment has gone. When the heat is at its hottest, we must deal with it in a way that will defuse the issue at hand, protecting ourselves, others, any property and the perpetrators. Our attitude must be the same as Christ's, being loving, respectful and forgiving. As in the case of the temple courtyard we must have our boundaries, and once those boundaries are crossed, then we must use our authority in dealing with the situation in the best and most lawful way we can.

Action page

Dealing with conflict: a summary

- Act with confidence.
- Defuse the situation immediately and don't let it grow into anything bigger.
- Do not meet aggression with aggression.
- Stand whenever possible right in the centre of the situation, though never have your back to anyone.
- Speak slowly and quietly, yet firmly. If you shout those involved will not respond or at least not as you may want them to. Shouting tells everyone that things are out of control. A firm quiet voice commands authority.
- Use your eyes for direct contact when speaking. Do not look to the ground or over their shoulder. Look straight at them, squarely in their eyes.
- Repeat what is being said, allowing them to hear back from you the key points of the problem as they see it. 'So you weren't doing anything to provoke Mark hitting you'. 'You feel that the toilet door being stiff for the last two months was unacceptable and taking it off its hinges seemed the best thing'. Repeating what is being said is very helpful for three reasons:
  ⇨ It slows down the intensity of the conflict.
  ⇨ It reassures the young person you are listening and taking them seriously.
  ⇨ Hearing what they have said summarised and repeated can help them get things into perspective. They may realise that things aren't as bad as they first thought or that their actions were unjustified.
- Give every opportunity for the individuals concerned to settle the problem. Allow them to leave feeling they have made the decision to cool it or resolve the issue for themselves. That way they have still saved face and been spared possible humiliation from peers.
- Don't issue directives: 'Leave now or I will call the police'. Try diversions: 'Do you think it would be a good idea to resolve the issue another time?' or: 'You know how reluctant I am to

involve the police, so how can we best settle the situation?' Directives are threatening. Contacting the police should be a last resort unless it is the only option available: for example if their actions are illegal or cannot be resolved without the aid of law enforcement.

- The minimum amount of fuss drawn to the scene the better. Attention can breath aggression. Always have leaders aware and nearby and able to help immediately but not directly involved. Leave the one leader to deal with it. A large presence of leaders circling around trouble can increase the hostility. Though common sense is required: a five foot lady in her fifties may need a hand breaking up a fight of eighteen-year-old boys.

PROBLEM
Broken lives

Category   *Child Abuse*

Symptoms   *Why does she avoid me like the plague?*
                   Why does he have bruises on top of bruises?
                   Does that lad really not possess any clean clothes?

Case History

Jennifer was fifteen and was considered to be very attractive by every boy in the group. She had a pale and fair complexion, but her skin often seemed blotchy. As a new recruit to the inner city Baptist Church youth group, Paul, the youth leader, had gone out of his way to make her feel at home among its thirty or so young members. But Jennifer had never responded too well to Paul, holding him at a distance and moving away whenever he came to talk to her. Initially, he thought she was shy, so he used all of his charm to win her over and build the good relationship with her that he enjoyed with every one else. This never happened. Feeling a little disappointed, he watched Jennifer during the meetings and was struck both by her poor body language and the fact that she only related well to females in the group. He felt this was odd, but he left it at that.

Some time later one of Jennifer's friends came to talk to Paul about the youth group going on a trip. As they discussed names and who would likely be able to attend, the girl, without any thought at all, dismissed the idea of Jennifer going, explaining that her dad was too strict. Since they had touched the subject Paul inquired a little more, wanting to know why Jennifer seemed so reserved. The girl paused for a moment and asked if Paul could keep something under his hat. He agreed. 'Don't take it personally', she said 'but Jennifer is afraid of men and so would I be if my father beat me each day!' Things then began to make sense to Paul.

'Does that explain her blotchy complexion?' he asked. 'That's when she has been crying, that's all', her friend replied. Then realising she had betrayed Jennifer's trust, she again begged him to keep the information to himself.

Care Plan

The subject of child abuse has become a buzz-word among youth leaders and church councils. New agendas are handed out with pages headed in bold print: 'Child protection policies', and with items for discussion such as 'All staff and volunteers should undergo police checks'; 'References required for all Sunday school teachers'; or 'No hugging of children'.

Congregations and youth ministries should welcome the acceptance of this responsibility by local leadership. It is sad that it is born after considerable delay and following many casualties. Child abuse has always been a reality, but with the growing demand for youth work, both church-based and in the community, the chances increase for youth leaders to come into contact with these fragile and broken young people more often.

What should we be aware of? The following list is not exhaustive.

- Abused young people may not be in every pew but abuse is both active and subtle. Child-line claimed some 9,097 children and young people had reported being sexually abused in just one year, 1994–5. Through 1998 some 30,000 children were placed on the 'Child Protection' register in England alone.
- Abuse is not usually carried out by an unknown 'weirdo'. Most of the time, the young person knows their abuser well, and they are family members, teachers or peers.
- Abuse is not always sexual or physical. A young person can be seriously damaged without ever being molested or beaten. The NSPCC claim at least one child dies each week through abuse and neglect.

- Abuse may well shame a young person into silence or even into defending the abuser.
- Absence of signs does not necessarily mean no abuse.

Most of us feel uneasy about the whole subject, hoping never to encounter a young victim of abuse. Questions such as 'How would I know?', 'What would I do?' or 'What happens if I get it wrong?' are in the forefront of our minds. Let's face it, no one wants to split a home or have a young person placed in care. In many cases this does not happen. A child may be removed from the environment, if it is considered they are in potential danger, while further investigation is undertaken. If a family unit can be preserved and spared from being broken up it will be. However the first and most important person must be the victim and their safety and support structure is vital.

Some of us may find ourselves in a similar dilemma to Paul, where the only way we can learn information is by exchanging a promise of secrecy. This should never happen, for the simple reason you must never be bound in issues of a person's safety or personal welfare. However confidentiality does not necessarily amount to secrecy.

Before we look at how or when we should react we need to be familiar with the different types of abuse.

Physical Abuse
Very simply, physical abuse occurs when a child is hurt by another person such as a parent or teacher or youth leader in a physical manner such as being punched, kicked, beaten with an object, shaken or thrown. These actions can result in cuts, bruises, fractured bones and can (rarely) lead to fatal consequences.

Sexual Abuse
This happens when a person is forced into a sexual experience either by an action or an environment. A person may be touched in areas regarded as sexual (breasts and genitals), or forced to have penetrative or oral sex including masturbation. They may have been forced to look at pornographic material on film or in

magazines, or even to watch others indulging in sexual behaviour. Give-away signs include a preoccupation with sexual matters, a tendency to provocative sexual behaviour, emotional withdrawal, nightmares, and various forms of anxious behaviour.

Emotional Abuse

This occurs when a person has been deprived of the most fundamental need we have in life: to be loved and accepted. Instead they may be criticised and generally told in word and actions they are of little or no importance. Instead of being praised for an action, they may be cursed and rejected. Peers also can be responsible for both emotional and physical abuse through bullying. Possible signs are that the person may suddenly start to underachieve at school, have a very poor sense of self worth, need continual affirmation from others, or seek attention at any cost.

Neglect

A person is neglected when they are no longer being cared for to the standard that they need. For example they may be underfed, shabby in appearance, lacking shelter and adequate warmth. Pointers may be injuries that are slow to heal and other health problems, mood swings and low esteem.

Spiritual

Spiritual abuses takes place when a person is forced to participate or believe in something. To a considerable degree, cults and some churches that practice heavy shepherding can remove a person's freedom to make decisions for themselves. This results in anxiety, frustration, a general fear of authority and other signs of indoctrination: an inability to make decisions, a preference for isolation, dependency on the group to which they belong and a hostility towards other churches.

Racial Abuse

This happens when a person is discriminated against, bullied or taunted for their ethnic origin, culture or colour. The victim may undergo many different types of abuse from bullying and harassment to other emotional and physical abuse. Racial abuse has both emotional and physical components.

In cases of racial and spiritual abuse, most social services are willing to accept them as forms of abuse but may not treat them in quite the same manner unless they involve physical, emotional, sexual or signs of neglect.

Having read through this list you might be forgiven for wondering if everyone in your group is suffering from some form of abuse. Another bruise on a fifteen year old male, a teenager who seems always to have a cough. . . . Most of the girls are riddled with feelings of inadequacy and low self esteem. Not to mention virtually every member in your group who leaves, feeling guilty after a strong Bible message. How can you differentiate these signs from true abuse? It's not easy.

In general what you are looking for are continuing signs and symptoms; their variety and their severity. However one bruise may be all you'll ever see, and you may well miss some abuse cases. Teenagers bruise themselves daily and to have to identify an injury as abuse instead of a sporting accident will be almost impossible for most of us. My suggestion is get to know your young people and what you don't know, find out. Remember always to apply common sense with caution and not assume abuse in all circumstances, because for 99 per cent of the time it won't be. But never be complacent in your thinking and attitude in case the 1 per cent that is abuse is happening to someone in your particular youth ministry.

What do I do if a young person tells me they are being abused?
Several years ago Youth For Christ considered this very issue and decided upon the following course of action:

- Look at the child directly.
- Accept everything the child says.
- Be aware that the child may have been threatened.
- Tell the child they are not to blame.

- Do not press for information.
- Reassure the child that they are right to tell you and you believe them.
- Let them know what you are going to do next, who you are going to tell and why, and roughly what will happen.
- Finish on a positive note.
- As soon as possible afterwards, make hand-written notes.

What do I do next?

- Evaluate the information – who told you, how do they know, did the person tell you directly? This is not an investigation but an exercise of clarity.
- Do not delay – If you have reason to suspect the person is in danger of harm in any of the five areas described above then do not leave the information another moment. Remember disclosed information cannot be kept confidential and you should never agree to secrecy.
- Do not hold the responsibility alone – be sure to involve others in your actions on a need-to-know basis. If possible meet the young person with someone else, but it must be someone with whom the young person must feel comfortable sharing such private details.
- Do not investigate any further – You could do considerably more damage by trying to piece information, facts and testimonies together or even trying to confront the offender. Leave it to the experts. In British law the responsibility for any investigation is with the social services, police or the NSPCC and it is not for workers to carry out these preliminary investigations.
- Consult with the leadership of the church or organisation – speak with your supervisor, if you have a breakdown in communications or if that particular individual is being considered as an abuser, then seek out another person in leadership.
- If the child is in immediate danger call the police on 999. If the abuse is not critical then contact the social services emergency duty officer or the police family protection unit. Either of these

numbers should be obtainable from directory inquiry. 'Not critical' should not mean delay!

It is your duty and responsibility to ensure the people in your care are indeed cared for. They may never thank you for it, you may be terrified of what will happen to them once it is out of your hands. However that is no longer your concern, but the concern of organisations and professionals whose job it is to ensure the young person is both out of any danger and cared for in the long term.

What will happen once a report is filed?
If one of the authorities mentioned above decides to act on an incident report, an investigation is likely to include

- An informal talk with the child
- A formal police or social services video recorded interview
- A medical examination (if appropriate)
- A preliminary family assessment

It is not unheard-of for a young person to 'cry wolf'. I have had it happen when a girl in my group accused her father of abuse. Her father, it turned out, was completely innocent. However, the question had to be asked why did she feel the need to make such accusations in the first place. Remember as far as abuse is concerned, the young person is always right until proved otherwise. As youth leaders we need also to be careful to protect ourselves from possible accusations. In a previous chapter, 'I think I'm in love with a member of my youth group!', I have given careful guidelines worth implementing if you do not have anything currently in place. I suggest you implement as a part of your policies the Government's guidelines, given on the Action page. If we want to protect our young people from risk then do not make the mistake of assuming youth leaders are risk-free. Have them checked out, screened and ensure they follow clear guidelines and roles within your ministries.

The Bible tells us that God loves us with an everlasting love (Jer. 31:3) and when Jesus said 'Let the children come to me', he looked upon those children with pure love, a love without limit or ending. It was never in his creation plan for a child to be abused in any way shape or form by an older or stronger person. When an abused child comes our way we must look upon them with the same eyes of love that he had. No matter how hurt or vulnerable they are, no matter how disgusting and inhuman the crime against them and no matter how filthy and low they may feel, nothing can keep that all-perfect love from them (Rom. 8:38,39). Jesus came to heal the broken-hearted. For some it may take a lifetime for him to achieve but he alone can soothe the pain and remove the memories.

Action Page

Adapted copy of the government recommendations for those working with children and young people in the voluntary sector as a result of the 1989 Children's Act.

Guideline 1 – Adopt a policy statement on safeguarding the welfare of children.

Guideline 2 – Plan the work of the organisation so as to minimise situations where the abuse of children may occur.

Guideline 3 – Introduce a system whereby children may talk with an independent person.

Guideline 4 – Apply agreed procedures for protecting children to all staff and volunteers.

Guideline 5 – Give all paid staff and volunteers clear roles.

Guideline 6 – Use supervision as a means of protecting children.

Guideline 7 – Treat all would-be paid staff as job applicants for any position involving contact with children.

Guideline 8 – Gain at least one reference from a person who has experience of the applicant's paid work or volunteering with children.

Guideline 9 – Explore all applicants' experience of working or contact with children in an interview before appointment.

Guideline 10 – Find out whether an applicant has any convictions for criminal offences against children.

Guideline 11 – Make paid and voluntary appointments conditional on the successful completion of a probationary period.

Guideline 12 – Issue guidelines on how to deal with the disclosure or discovery of abuse.

Guideline 13 – Train paid staff and volunteers, their line managers or supervisors and policy makers in the prevention of child abuse.

If you find these guidelines both practical and responsible then sign below that you will adhere to them. Consult either your church or organisation if they do not have such a policy in place.

I, ..., agree to all 13 guidelines and will adhere to each step mentioned. I will also consult with the church/organisation I work for to ensure they have a similar policy in place.

Signed . . . .   Date . . . .

Please note all guidelines throughout this chapter are based upon experienced organisations and government policies and procedures. Although I have received training in this area and, sadly, have some experience in helping abused young people, I wouldn't regard myself as an expert and I would encourage any youth leader working with young people to attend one or more 'Child protection' courses which you will find both informative and helpful. Both secular (such as the social services) and Christian agencies run such events frequently and locally.

Much appreciation to Youth for Christ for their helpful contribution of resources on this issue.

PROBLEM
I've got a school assembly, what do I do?

Category   *Schools work*

Symptoms   *The idea you had for praying for all the sick people in the hall and casting out evil spirits was not well received by the headmaster.*
You were recently laughed off stage for being a corny religious nut!
You can't come up with any good ideas so you stay in bed pretending to be sick.

Case History

The local year out team finished the assembly in prayer. It had been a good message but had lasted for no more than two minutes. The dragon-like head of year thanked them for the assembly and went on to talk about the issue raised. After eight minutes or so, she finished by praying and dismissed the year group. Turning to the team she summoned them to her room. Closing the door behind her she looked at the three youth workers and said she was wondering why they had bothered to turn up that morning? All they had done was to introduce the theme and left her to take the assembly. 'Next time give it a bit more thought will you?' They apologised and crept out.

Care Plans

You put the phone down. It was the local secondary school head of year – inviting you into the school to discuss the possibility of doing an assembly. At last you finally have an entry. But now you begin to wonder: 'What have I got to offer; what do they expect of me?'

The 1988 Religious Reform Act, which requires schools to be involved in daily acts of predominantly Christian worship, can open a door which normally would be closed. However, the majority of schools are very cautious when it comes to trusting members of the community, and religious ones at that, with their precious pupils. Our image, agenda, message and presentation has to be the best it can possibly be. In my experience most secondary schools are unable to achieve the legal requirement mainly because it is not practically possible. Often they do not have staff with conviction or expertise in this area. If the assembly is a success, the likelihood is you will become a regular visitor helping them to provide some form of Christian worship. My busiest time with schools has been around Ofsted inspections. So be warned!

When you have the preliminary meeting with the school officials, think through carefully what you wish to present, because unless the head is a raving evangelical it is unlikely they will welcome a straight-for-the-jugular 'Repent or burn' message. Most schools welcome religious assemblies with a strong slant towards moral issues. Teachers are all too aware how morally bankrupt many young people of today are; with no role models or positive examples they have little chance of being anything else. Suitable themes might include

- Absolutes
- Bullying
- Values
- Forgiveness
- Self-esteem
- Relationships
- Love
- Money
- Racial differences
- Drugs, drink and rock'n'roll
- Family

Around the time of festivals you have a better opportunity to be more bold in the message you give

- Christmas – Light enters the world
- Easter – Jesus dies for mankind
- Pentecost – Holy Spirit impacts the world
- Harvest – God provides for our needs

Once we become accepted within the school, then we may be allowed to be a bit more adventurous. Teachers need to know they can trust you before you start leading assemblies on belief, salvation, creation, life after death and so on.

You have had your meeting and you took your diary (something I once forgot – very embarrassing!). They liked your ideas and could see you weren't out to convert the school, at least not during the first assembly. They have given you a trial assembly in two weeks time. Big time panic, what do you do?

The Assembly: How to do it!

Choose a theme: Once you have your theme, think hard about the point you want to make. In such a short period of time, talking to young people who may not be sympathetic to the gospel, it is essential we are very simple in our approach. Take one theme and make one point only. For example, if the theme is self-worth, the one point you want to make is our value does not come from our appearance or our intellect or our talents but from deep within (the heart).

Be visual: It is important to make your presentation attractive and fairly fast-moving. One moment you are talking, the next you are showing something, then you are making a mess. Be creative in visual presentations, and make sure you are in a good place to be seen.

Use volunteers: Help from a member of the audience can add to the excitement of the presentation especially if the audience is unsure what is going to happen to the volunteer. Always look after your volunteers, avoid humiliating them and make sure they come to no harm. To my shame I once led an assembly where a volunteer was to fall backwards and be caught; the catcher, who was a competent member of staff, was day dreaming when the volunteer fell and the catcher didn't catch!

Use drama and dramatic readings: Good, creative drama can capture the audience, especially if it emphasises the point. Good drama makes the difference between an OK assembly and an excellent one.

Emphasise the one point in many different ways: Though we may only make one point which could be said in one sentence, the assembly will last a lot longer than a sentence. Any good communicator keeps his points simple and makes the same point again and again using illustrations, stories, visual aids and verbal explanations to highlight clearly what is being said.

Be on time: Late arrivals stress teachers, late team members stress the rest of the team and look sloppy and unprofessional. I have had members of my team turn up half way through the assembly. If you have unreliable staff then you have to be prepared to wing it!

Don't go over time: Never let the bell for the end of the assembly ring while you are still talking. Anything you have said and done that morning will be lost. Even if the teacher instructs the pupils to sit still and wait until you finish, the reality is they are thinking about their next class. However, do use the time you have, because teachers hate having to improvise because you finished far too early, as in the example mentioned earlier. Assemblies are given a certain amount of time that must be filled and no one can leave until the bell goes. So you should make the most use of this time, but remember that most teachers like to have a minute at the end to give out announcements.

Enjoy yourself: The more you relax and enjoy the assembly the more the audience will join you. If you are tense and rigid the likely response from the audience will be the same.

End in prayer: Ask the school if they mind you closing in prayer. Be daring and ask the teacher in charge of the assembly if there are any particular issues or prayer needs that are relevant for you to pray about.

School ministry has always been the stepping-stone to further outreach. When you see pupils in the schools through assembly, lunch clubs, lessons and after school activities frequently those relationships can develop to out of school activities such as drop ins, missions and Church youth group activities. Schools work fulfils an immediate goal as well as long term objectives.

Action page

Assembly on Value

Prepare   A bag with 5 or 6 objects inside it
2 balloons of the same size and shape

Start the assembly with a bag of objects that you have recently bought and know exactly how much you paid for them. Ask for a volunteer to come and help you. Tell the volunteer you will show them an object and he or she has to guess how much the object cost. Example – a Bic pen. The volunteer estimates a figure '99p'. Then you hold the pen to the audience and ask people to vote. They have three votes and can only use their vote once. 'If it is higher than 99p raise your hands . . .' wait for hands and then ask them to lower once you have a rough idea. 'if it is lower than 99p raise your hands . . .'. 'If it is the same as 99p raise your hands . . .'. Then tell the audience how much it actually cost. Have about five objects and repeat the exercise, encouraging a quiz-show atmosphere. Once you have gone through the items, thank the volunteer and ask the audience to give him or her a clap. It is a good idea to reward your volunteers with a Mars bar or equivalent. Go on to make the point 'This morning we are going to discuss value'.

Tell them they have just made an evaluation of how much something is worth, and explain they do it every day, from choosing the clothes they wear, to making priority values. For instance, when they go home they can decide either to play on the Play Station first or do their home work. Explain that every day they are also making evaluations about people. When you pick the football team the person you pick first is the person you value to be the best of the line-up. You evaluate who is your best friend and who is your worst enemy. People also make the same decisions about you. They decide how much you are worth by your appearance, your skills, your character, your academic ability and your personality.

Then ask the question 'If I'd brought you up to the front and asked how much you were worth, how much do you think the audience would have estimated your value at? £10 or £100, maybe £1000, perhaps you think more or perhaps you think less?'

At this point use an example of when you or someone you know may have felt worthless when valued in such materialistic ways. . . . Then go on to point out that you have learned your value does not come from your appearance or your social background, how good you are at sports or how clever you are in the class room. Your value is found in something altogether very different.

Ask for two volunteers – one male and one female. Give each volunteer one of the balloons. On the word 'go' they are to compete to blow up the largest balloon. Divide the room and tell all the girls they have to shout and cheer for the female volunteer and all the boys have to shout and cheer for the male. Obviously one balloon will eventually burst. Wait until one bursts and then thank the volunteers, giving a reward to both. Encourage a loud and robust environment, but not so robust that you can't calm them down afterwards.

Go on to paraphrase the story of Samuel choosing David as King – by explaining in detail how his other brothers looked more attractive, clever, great personalities, warrior potential but God chose an immature lad. Why?

Read 1 Samuel 16:7

Make the point, going back to the balloons, that earthly value is completely empty. A person's true worth is not in their appearance, or their figure, nor is it found in their skill. Valuing others or ourselves according to how we look, how we talk, and what we can do, is to undervalue us. It is an empty valuation – like the balloon. And, as when the balloon burst, such a valuation can be destructive. It unbalances us – mentally, emotionally and spiritually and possibly physically as well.

'God does not judge your earthly appearance or ability – He loves everyone so much that He gave His Son to die on the cross for us. But He does judge your heart and when He looks at you He looks for signs of our love for Him. To Him you are priceless. There is no value tag on you because you are worth too much. In reality who would you most like to be valued by – your parents, your teachers, your friends, your enemies or God?' Let's pray. . . .

The 1988 Religious Reform Act is continually being discussed in Parliament and may be changed. At the time of going to print, this Act was very much in force.

PROBLEM
Am I really expected to encourage my youth group in street evangelism?

Category   *Outreach*

Symptoms   *No one in the group thinks bashing people with Bibles is very trendy or helpful.*
Some of the boys think street work is a chance to pick up a chick.
The group have decided that until they have an Acts 2 experience they should stay firmly off the streets.

Case History

The group of trainee youth workers had been assigned to put together an effective open-air outreach programme. Needless to say they were excited by it. After twenty minutes or so they approached me with their ideas and asked what I thought. I wasn't so convinced but reluctantly said they could have a go. Experience was the main thing here and I knew they would get it. Their plan was for two people to have a disagreement in the street and then let it grow into a full-blown domestic incident. Once a crowd had begun to take interest, they would then start to speak to the crowd about love and Jesus, followed by sketches and other great ideas.

In the small Midlands town, the group raced out of the building with plenty of enthusiasm and took up position. I decided to watch from afar. Two of the group started arguing loudly in the centre of a busy shopping precinct and before long they were screaming at each other about whom they had or hadn't slept with. A crowd materialised and I watched anxiously, hoping they would soon stop. No one would have guessed this was only an act and not a real life row!

Out of the corner of my eye I noticed an odd looking character walking towards them, carrying what looked like a bottle of spirits. He was heading straight for the male actor who was called John. I though it best I move closer. Before John knew anything about it the stranger was upon him. He started to shout at John, demanding he should shut up and show greater respect to his girl friend. John ignored him and carried on the argument. The man, who was obviously drunk, did not like being ignored and gave him a mouthful of curses and threats. John became a little distracted but did not stop. At this point I knew their plan was failing; the best one could hope for was that they might escape embarrassed but unharmed. Just when it looked like things had got completely out of control and the man had begun to wave his fist in John's face, I made my move, rushing both John and the girl off the scene. As we were leaving a police car pulled up and two officers made their way to the precinct. I had no intention of hanging around. Later several members of the church who had seen the incident, phoned to let me know how disgusted they were that members of my team had been arguing in front of a crowd about their sexual exploits.

Care Plans

When it comes to street evangelism, young people can be very enthusiastic. Yet both for their safety and for the credibility of the Gospel it has to be done well. Many leaders are unsure what to do when members of their group show an active interest in street work and detached evangelism. Other leaders have lots of ideas but their young people are not enthusiastic, being too concerned about their image and who may be embarrassed to see them patrolling the streets.

We should encourage detached outreach or open air evangelism by our youth groups for several reasons.

- Proactive evangelism is Biblical. The whole ethos of sharing our faith with others should be central to our teaching in our fellowship groups. When Jesus sent out the twelve or seventy-two, he commissioned them to go from town to town 'Freely you have received, freely give'. In Acts 1:8 he urged the apostles to be his witnesses, first in Jerusalem (their home town) then in Samaria and Judea (surrounding neighbours), then to the ends of the earth. The book of Acts clearly illustrates that being a witness was not merely an ideal to be demonstrated in the work place and at home, but much more; it was to be a proactive verbal proclamation, accompanied both by a life-style and gifts inspired by the Holy Spirit. The examples of Peter preaching to the thousands and Paul continually travelling to preach about Christ show clearly that there should be an aggressive aspect to evangelism.

- Evangelism should be a positive experience. After our teaching we should offer opportunities for members of the group to be involved actively in sharing their faith. Otherwise we are telling them they must do something but we are not helping them in a constructive way to achieve it. Remember evangelism for most people is unnatural; they want to do it but have no idea how.

- Evangelism is a great way to learn more about yourself and your own faith. Taking people on to the streets to talk to their peers about what they believe challenges the young apologist to think even deeper about what he or she believes. An evangelist who worked for YfC several years ago would only take non-believers on the streets with him. The young people who had been approached would eventually turn from the evangelist to his companion and ask him what he believed – it wasn't long before the young friend of the evangelist came to his own faith. I'm not suggesting you should take non-believers or fringe believers with you: I'm merely pointing out that evangelism can challenge the giver just as much as the receiver.

Once we are committed to street outreach then we need to consider seriously the following two points:

- Safety. When you take the youth group onto the streets, you must ensure the supervision is good. Not only should it be a

positive experience but a safe experience. With the right super-vision and the right environment (e.g. not Friday night after the clubs shut), then the young people can freely experiment, without worrying about their own personal security.
- Evangelism should be effective. When you send your group onto the streets ensure you have given them teaching on what to do, what to say, what not to say, how to act, how to relate, how to pray for someone, use of tracts if you have them, what contact address should be given, and details of any follow-up plans. If you or members of your church cannot provide this teaching, then consider approaching missionary organisations who are experienced in outreach and would be willing to visit and lead a training day. (Organisations such as YfC, or YWAM are just two examples. A full list can be found in the UK Christian Handbook).

Having been involved with teaching young people in evangelism for several years, I have come to realise if it's done correctly, street work can be great fun, with lots of laughs afterwards and sur-prises. The boldest members of your group may fall at the first hurdle, while the quieter ones may well come alive. There are mainly two types of street outreach, public (open air campaign) or detached. Public outreach is aimed at attracting the crowds by using entertaining methods such as sketch boards, drama, music, juggling, magic or flame throwing, followed with a short punchy message. At the same time, members of the group mingle with the crowd, taking opportunities to talk one-to-one. Detached evange-lism is less public and involves two or three people walking the streets and approaching people. The detached workers build a rapport and are then able to share their faith, or can invite people to a planned event the church may be running. With first timers, questionnaires can help in breaking the ice. Carefully chosen questions can give confidence to the individual asking them, a clearer excuse for stopping people and can also give some direc-tion to subsequent conversations. With experience, 'cold stopping' without questionnaires can be much more rewarding in terms of seeing interest develop beyond the first stages.

In addition, continuity is vital in detached work – taking young people regularly to areas where relationships have developed with those they have talked to in the past can be very valuable.

The whole aim of detached evangelism or public outreach is to tell people about Jesus and bring them to some form of living faith. It is crucial that every one involved understands what they are about, understands their own faith enough both to be able to present their belief in a relaxed and attractive way and also to share it in such a way that it attracts others to this faith.

Jesus said 'As the Father has sent me, therefore I send you'. (Jn. 20:21) Evangelism is central to the Gospel message. For some, public or detached youth work may not be where they are most theologically or socially comfortable. For others it's an ideal way of training up young evangelists to be active in their faith. Many leaders exhort their young people to evangelise and may even tell them how many people they must share the gospel with by next week, yet they only frustrate members of their group because they never really offer practical help. Suppose my father, when I reached seventeen, told me I had a week to learn how to drive, gave me the car keys and said: 'Off you go'. I might have smashed the car, killed a few old ladies, even knocked a few telegraph poles down but I doubt I'd have really known how to drive a week later.

Jesus demonstrated to his disciples, stood beside them and watched. Then he stood back and allowed them to do it on their own. We need to firstly show, then stand with them and finally when they are ready let them freely share without our help or supervision. Training young people to bring others to faith and helping them as they are attempting it is no small matter. Let us put evangelism high on our agendas and make opportunities for young people to learn and grow as evangelists and witnesses within the community.

Action page

Self Examination

🎬 If you are thinking of taking your group on to the streets then think through the following issues:

- Is the group ready for public evangelism?

- Does the group understand the Gospel enough to share it clearly and effectively?

- Have you provided training for the group in how to share their faith creatively, how to open and close a conversation and how to pray for an individual to come to faith?

- What plans do you have for follow-up after interest has been shown?

- Do you intend to use any forms of tract? If so, is the group confident in using them and are the tracts relevant?

- Are members of the group able to give their testimony to class mates or to unknown peers?

- What safety precautions are you taking, e.g. how many leaders, what time of day etc?

- Are parents aware of the event, if involving minors?

- If you are involved in detached evangelism, how many are going in a team and have you the correct mix of workers? (e.g. two very confident people together or two very shy unsure people may not work)

- How well do you know the area; do young people hang out around that area; what information do you have on the street's young people?

- Have you informed the police and clearly identified your workers with ID?

- Do you have people praying while you are out?

PROBLEM
I can't be expected to practise everything I preach can I?

Category   *Credibility and integrity of the youth leader*

Symptoms   *Log starts to shoot from your eye.*
Find members of your youth group hiding in your garden with cameras and note books.
Given the golden award for being the most totally unachievable role model.

Case History

Scott was in his mid-thirties and was the senior youth pastor for a large church on the south coast of the United States. Each Sunday afternoon over 300 fourteen- to eighteen-year-olds would meet together for worship and Bible teaching, which Scott would usually lead.

This particular Sunday, Scott's wife had been taken ill, so she was unable to take care of their daughter Jesse while youth fellowship was on. Reluctantly Scott had to take the apple of his eye to the meeting. He found a corner in the room for Jesse to sit quietly and play with a selection of toys while he preached to his vibrant congregation. After the worship, he got to his feet, flung open his Bible and preached an eloquent, entertaining yet at times sharp message on servanthood. When he came to the point of being a servant at home, putting aside selfishness and being at all times sacrificial, he gave clear and visual illustrations, such as washing the dishes, cleaning the kitchen, brushing the toilet and helping with the meals. Scott was stopped in his tracks when his five-year-old daughter, who had been listening intently, decided enough was enough. She stood up and spoke as loudly as she could: 'Daddy, if Mummy heard what you were saying, she would be very angry because you never help around the house. Mummy works so hard while you say you're always too tired or you need to read the paper or watch the TV'.

The preacher was speechless. His little girl had noticed what he was like at home and scolded him in public for pretending to be something else.

Care Plans

The person you are in your private life should be the same person you are in your public life. Most of us are fortunate not to be contradicted by members of our families, but often in the depth of our souls something does not rest easy. Many of us are faced with teaching our young people on almost every subject under the sun. Yet when we reach subjects like holiness, righteous living, prayer, the urgency of reading our Bible, witnessing, sin, or relationships, we are bound to find them a struggle to present if we are struggling with them in our own lives. Most of us (if not all of us) do not claim to have our Christian lifestyles at the standard the Bible instructs us. Therefore we must be careful not to be perceived as judging others in our teaching on any subject we ourselves have not mastered, otherwise is it not a case of looking at the speck in another's eye but ignoring the log in our own? (Matt. 7:3–5).

If we are truthful, then we must admit that we often live a different message to the one we preach. Our private life at times really does not match our public life. It may in most areas, but probably not all. The need to be seen as the one who has it all together, the one who does not struggle, the one who is in constant dialogue with his Maker is a foolish trap. Involvement in ministry makes us believe these are the standards we must achieve and these are the expectations people have of us. The reality for most people in ministry is often far from this. Many youth leaders and many ministers are riddled with guilt because they are often trapped by the message they preach.

Here is the good news. Young people aren't looking for perfect leaders or perfect role models, they are wanting leaders who are real. Leaders who know what it is like to fail and so won't shout at them when they fall. Leaders who don't heap so much guilt on the group that they lose any sense of worth. Young people want a leader who comes alongside and can say: 'It's hard and I haven't got it right yet!' They want leaders who can pick them up, who can encourage them and who can inspire them.

The bad news is that if the standards you set for your group are too high and the image you portray of yourself is of someone who has attained it all, then every move you make is watched. If you fail or if they sense you are not being truthful, then you will lose their confidence and belief in you, and the credibility of what you say in the future may well be questioned.

Our aim is to be more like Christ, to put away the things of the flesh and only live for the things of God. Holiness is not an over-night achievement, it involves time, failures, pruning and an endless amount of wrestling with what is right and what is wrong (Jn. 15:2). The renewing of the mind is something we must desire first before we can succeed (Rom. 12:2). Don't be too hard then on yourself or those in your group who haven't yet reached that all-perfect example of Jesus. Holiness is not so much the action that attains the achievement, but the attitude that desires the achievement. We are made perfect in Christ, through Jesus' death (Rom. 5:8,9) and where sin reigns grace reigns all the more (Rom. 5:20,21). I personally think reaching a stage in life where we no longer fail may actually be out of our grasp at this moment in time, for what we see and have now is only a dim reflection of what will come, though a time is coming when it will be achieved (1 Cor. 13:8–12). However, this is no excuse for us to hold back from trying and daily allowing Jesus to renew and refine a new area in our lives. As Paul urges, despite our past we should press on to reach the goal and win the prize (Phil. 3:12–14).

When you speak on a subject that you haven't mastered, don't give the impression you have. Tell them you struggle and are still working through it. Don't hang your dirty washing out for all to see and don't so expose yourself that you lose all credibility. If you have got the better of an issue such as finding time each day to read your Bible, try to be honest and say you didn't always find it so easy and perhaps at times you still don't. I am not suggesting failing to read your Bible is sinful, but for spiritual growth is an absolute. If there is a subject that you haven't remotely cracked and are failing more than you are winning, then ask another leader to speak on it, who perhaps can give more positive and clearer practical guidance on the subject than you can. There is no shame in handing issues over: it's more important they receive good input than something that sounds unconvincing.

It's a fact of life that we warm far more to those who are honest, than to those who seem to be so perfect they are too far removed for us ever to draw close to them. Your honesty and your humility will bring major blessings and fruit to the lives of young people. Be real, be humble and be approachable.

Action page

Reaching perfection as a leader

• How can Matthew 7:1–5 be applied to people in positions of leadership?

• In Philippians 3:10–14, what can we learn about Paul as regards perfection and what is his attitude towards his objectives?

• What does James 3:1,2 say in relation to leaders and teachers?

• Look at 1 John 1:8,9. This is a reality check – why is it important and how does it apply to us as leaders?

PROBLEM
Am I supposed to be a spiritual guru?

Category   *Spiritual role models*

Symptoms   *The young people announce they wish to join a monastery and shave their heads bald because they desire the same spirituality as their leader.*
You're wondering why they smile so cynically when you get up to preach.
Books on basic Christianity appear on your doorstep together with invites to Alpha courses.

Case History

Jim had been one of the youth leaders for the Baptist church in the Dales for many years. The church had been short of leaders for a considerable amount of time and Jim, though perhaps not ideal, was always willing. Along with the two other faithful church youth leaders, he was responsible for the spiritual teaching of the fifteen regular teenagers in the group.

One evening, Jim announced to the group they would study the subject of prayer. Turning to the fifteen or so thirteen- to sixteen-year-olds, he declared: 'If I'm really honest, then I should tell you I never pray, other than on a Sunday when in church, of course.'

The group was silent, unsure how to take this confession. Jim continued: 'So, rather than having me blabber on this evening, I want you to get into groups and discuss the questions on the sheets about Jesus teaching the disciples to pray.' After there had been some feedback from the sheets, Jim went on to ask the group if they had any further questions. One bright fourteen-year-old boy asked Jim to explain the difference between 'contemplative prayer' and 'meditative prayer'. With a deep frown on his face Jim replied: 'I don't know, any other questions?' There was a moment of silence, then the same boy raised his hand and asked Jim to explain the difference between 'liturgical prayer' and 'mystical prayer'. Jim gave out a loud sigh and asked the boy to be more constructive with his questions. The boy was straight back on the man's heels and said: 'Jim, if you don't pray and you don't know anything about prayer, then why are you teaching us about prayer?'

Care Plans

It's already been pointed out that we aren't expected to have all the answers to questions, nor to have mastered all areas of our lives. We're all on a journey which lasts a lifetime! However there are certain aspects in our own personal spiritual lives which, if lacking in depth, will result in our teaching being at a very shallow level. Jim was teaching on a subject about which he had neither experience nor any academic or theological insight. Jesus refers to a situation not too dissimilar to Jim's with the Pharisees when he describes them as the 'blind leading the blind' (Mt. 15:14).

As spiritual leaders it is vital that we are committed to our own personal spiritual growth for three important reasons

- We should only instruct others in issues of faith to which we are committed. If we are not committed to these areas, but still teach them, then we are being hypocritical. 'Don't do as I do but do as I say I do!'
- We can only lead people as far as we have been ourselves. Jim couldn't talk on prayer as he had no real experience or understanding of it. To lead others we must have walked that path beforehand. If we haven't been there, we are likely to have no more insight than those who are following us and that really becomes a case of the blind leading the blind.
- The example we are setting should be a positive one. Young people look for role models. Many times they will accept your

example, whether it be right or wrong. 'Bill doesn't read his Bible. That's OK – so I don't have to'. 'Jenny only goes to church when she feels like it; that's great, I can lie in on Sunday'.

Some of us may be feeling uncomfortable at this moment, realising our spiritual journey is patchy and inconsistent. Perhaps you're feeling a weight descending upon you, the one you thought the chapter 'I can't be expected to practise everything I preach can I?' had removed. The good news is that it's far more important to our spiritual leadership that we continually pursue holiness and a deeper intimacy with God, rather than getting hung up on patchy prayer times, the occasional lapsed Bible study and disjointed fellowships. We may not reach our goal each day, but as long as we continually desire it and our experiences of God do not become mere fading memories, then we won't find ourselves leading groups in the dark, not knowing which direction to take.

For the spiritual welfare of the group, it is more important we have more spiritual maturity and depth to our faith than the average fifteen-year-old attending church. That is not to disrespect the spirituality of young people but to suggest that our own spirituality must have some maturity. Why? Because Jesus said a 'student can only become as great as his master or teacher'. (Lk.6:40) If we are spiritually shallow then the very best our young people can ever expect to grow into is shallowness.

Yet if we have an active faith that is committed to a living intimate relationship with God and a theologically based belief, then we will continually grow and so will the depth we have to communicate, and on that basis so will the young people who follow. A youth leader's love for the Lord can become infectious. If they can see it in you, then they will be drawn in and desire the same love for God. As a leader you have the most amazing opportunity to nurture young people into an active, intimate and radical relationship with God. It's every youth worker's dream for their group to be sold-out for God. It's every youth worker's dream to brag of how often the young people pray, fast, read their Bibles, hold night-long worship events, patrol the streets sharing their faith, and give beyond measure to the poor and needy. Much of the key to achieving this is in the relationship you have with God and how much of that they can see coming across in your teaching, pastoral care and contact with them. The simple path to growth within your group is by teaching them from experience and example. 'Do as I do!'

Action page

What kind of spiritual guru am I?

- How often do I pray?
  Daily – 4 or 5 times a week – 1 or 2 times a week
  Hardly ever
  Never

- How often do I study my Bible?
  Daily – 4 or 5 times a week – 1 or 2 times a week
  Hardly ever
  Never

- How often do I attend Church?
  2 or 3 times a week
  Once a week
  Once every 2 weeks
  Once every month
  Once in a blue moon

- How much prayer do I put into the teaching I give to the young people?
  A lot – Some – A little – None

- How much biblical research do I make in preparation to my teaching?
  A lot – Some – A little – None

- How often do I speak on issues when I know I have not yet walked that path, or that I have very limited experience to share on the subject?
  Almost every time I lead
  Every other time I lead
  It happens
  Rarely happens
  Never happens

- If a young person could see into my spiritual life what kind of example would I be setting?
  Very positive – Good – Not so good – Very poor

- What areas do you need to work on for your own growth and so that young people can achieve the growth you want them to achieve?

Additional resources

Books, organisations and further places for help

For chapters that cover many of the issues given below, try *The Christian Youth Manual*, Steve Chalke, Kingsway 1992, and *Worship and Youth Culture*, Pete Ward, Marshall Pickering 1993, and *Jesus for a New Generation*, Kevin Ford, Hodder and Stoughton. Other books concentrating on youth are John Buckeridge's *The Youthwork Handbook*, Kingsway 1996 and *Saving the Millennial Generation* by Dawson McAllister with Pat Springle, Nelson 1999. *How to stay sane when your family is cracking* up by Colin Piper, Chris Curtis and Tim Dobson, Scripture Union 1993, sets out to help children and young people whose families are falling apart.

A good resource that appears each month is Youthwork magazine. For details contact CCP, Glen House, Stag Place, London.

Chapter 1: *How can I have a successful youth ministry?*

The Best of Power Pack, Bob Moffett

Teach the Bible Creatively, Bill McNab & Steve Mckay: Youth Specialties/Zondervan

Keep 'em talking, Mike Yaconelli: Youth Specialties/Zondervan 1997

Case Studies, talk sheets & discussion starters, Jim Burns & Mark Simone: Gospel Light 1997

Speak up with Confidence, Carol Kent: Nav Press 1997

Have you ever?, Les Christies: Youth Specialties/Zondervan 1998

Quick help! Best ever ideas for youth ministry, published anonymously by Group 1997.

All star games for all star youth leaders, published anonymously by Group publishers 1998

The youthworkers ideas depot: 1001 greatest ideas of youth ministry, CD Rom Group 1997

Chapter 2: **How important are numbers?**
Young people and small groups, Danny Brierely

Help I'm a small group leader, Laurie Polich: Youth Specialties/ Zondervan 1998

Small group resources (Vols 1 & 2), Bo Boshers and the student impact team: Zondervan 1997

Small group outreach, Jeffrey Arnold: Intervarsity press1998

Big ideas for small youth groups, Patrick Angier & Nick Allen: Marshall Pickering 1993

Chapter 3: **How do I know when things are going off the rails?**
Understanding teenagers, Pete Gilbert 1993

Programming with purpose, Troy Murthy with Kim Anderson: Zondervan 1997

Fourth cycle Student Ministry, Mark de Ymaz: Fellowship Student Ministries 1997

Chapter 4: **Not the youth weekend again?**
Ideas: camps, retreats, missions and service ideas, Youth Specialties/Zondervan 1997/8

Take 'em away, Nick Harding

Time Out, Kieran Sawyer: Ave Maria Press 1998

Chapter 5: **Why don't members of my group change and resemble Christians?**
Get real, Mal Fletcher: Word 1993

What would Jesus do? Spiritual Challenge Journal, Mike Yaconelli: Youth Specialties/Zondervan 1997

Leading teens to freedom to Christ, Neil T Anderson & Rich Miller: Regal books 1997

Chapter 6: Is faith inherited or chosen?
Growing up Evangelical, Pete Ward SPCK

Chapter 7: How can I get members of my youth group to attend church?
Worship Ideas for Youth Ministry, anonymous, published by Group 1997

Christian Youth Work, Mark Ashton & Phil Moon: Monarch

The church and youth ministry, Edited by Pete Ward: Lynx

Church: why bother?, Philip Yancey: Zondervan 1998

Youth ministry in a box, Rodney J Mills: Youth box production 1998

Chapter 8: How can I get my youth group to pray?
Serious prayer, Trevor Gregory: Scripture Union 1997

NYPD – National Youth Prayer Diary, CPAS

Bill Hogg's Most Excellent Guide to Prayer, Bill Hogg Kingsway 1992 (sadly out of print but you might find it secondhand somewhere).

Take hold of life: A quiet time journal for teens, Sheila Jones: Discipleship Publications International 1997

Prayer Services for Young Adolescents, Gwen Costello: Twenty-Third Publications

20 more teen prayer services, S Kevin Regan: Twenty-Third Publications

Chapter 9: How do I deal with teenage self-esteem
Pastoral care for young people, Mark Vernon

Understanding today's youth culture, Walt Mueller: Tyndale 1994

Identity in Adolescence, Jane Kroger: Routledge 1996

Adolescent Gambling, Mark Griffiths: Routledge 1995

When nothing matters any more; A survival guide for depressed teens, Bev Cobain: Free Spirit 1998

Ministry with youth in crisis, Harley Atkinson: Religious education press 1997

Childline Tel: 0800 1111

Samaritans 0345 909090 (for local branch, see entry in your
telephone directory)
Counselling: CWR, Waverley Abbey House, Waverley Lane,
Farnham, Surrey GU9 8EP Tel: 01252 783695

Chapter 10: **Is the media and the music world of the Devil?**
Music worth talking about, Tim & Patty Atkins: Baker Book
House/STL
Chart watch, Bob Smithouser & Bob Waliszewski: Tyndale 1998
Truth about rock, Steve Peters & Mark Littleton: Bethany House
1998

Chapter 11: **I think I'm in love with a member of my youth group!**
*Overcoming the dark side of leadership: the paradox of personal
dysfunction*, Gary L McIntosh & Samuel D Rima Sr: Baker
1997

Chapter 12: **When is sex right?**
And God created Sex!, Chick Yuill: Monarch
Am I in love?, Karen Dockrey: Concordia 1997
Me, you, us, them, CYPAS
What Hollywood won't tell you about sex, love and dating, Greg
Johnson and Susie Shellenberger: Regal Books 1994
AIDS helpline, PO Box 1577, London NW1 3DW Tel: 0171 387
6900
Sex Matters, Steve Chalke and Nick Page: Hodder and Stoughton
Parents first – sex education within the home, Resource manual
from CARE

Chapter 13: **How do I deal with that teenage crush?**
Any of the books recommended for the Chapter on teenage
self-esteem may help give an insight as to what is going on here.

Chapter 14: **I'm not sure I'm cut out for this?**
So that's why I keep doing this, Glen Procopio: Youth Specialties/
Zondervan 1998

Purpose-driven Youth ministry, Doug Fields: Youth Specialties/
  Zondervan 1998
*When Kumbaya is not enough – a practical theology for youth
  ministry*, Dean Borgman: Hendrick publishers 1997
What I wish my youth leader knew about youth ministry, Mike
  Nappa: Standard 1999

Chapter 15: **What do I do with the leaders I have?**
Developing the Leader within you, John C Maxwell: Word
  1993
Making a team work, Steve Chalke with Penny Relph: Kingsway
  1998
Pulling together – the power of team work, John J Murphy:
  Wynwood 1997

Chapter 16: **Is fifteen too young to be a leader?**
Empowering students to transform schools, Gary Goldman &
  Jay B Newman: Corwin Press 1998
Leaders are learners, Doug Fields (Cassette: 714/459–9517)

Chapter 17: **Do parents go to hell?**
Twenty hot potatoes that Christians are afraid to touch, Tony
  Campolo: Word
*Sceptics answered: Handling tough questions about the Christian
  faith*, D James Kennedy: Multomah 1997
True for you but not for me, Paul Copan: Bethany House 1998
Don't check your brains at the door, Josh McDowell & Bob
  Hostetler: Word 1992
Right from wrong, Josh McDowell & Bob Hostetler: Word

Chapter 18: **Am I really expected to take on the family as well as the young person?**
Understanding today's youth culture, Walt Mueller: Tyndale
  1994 (for parents to read).
Preparing to parent teenagers, Paul Scott Evans: Paternoster 1999
*The influential parent: how to be the person your teen really
  needs*, David Damico: Shaw 1997

Staying friends with your kids, Kathy Collard Millar & Dancy
Millar: Shaw 1997
The youth-workers handbook to family ministry, Chap Clark:
Youth Specialties/Zondervan
Baker handbook of single parent ministry, Bobbie Reed: Baker 1998

Chapter 19: How do I deal with pranks?
Struggling with reality, Brainstormers Video 1995

Chapter 20: He only broke his arm!
Theme Games, Lesley Pinchbeck
Games without Frontiers, Pip Wilson: Marshall Pickering 1988
Crowd breakers Books 1 & 2, Bob Moffett: Marshall Pickering
Over 300 Games for all Occasions, Patrick Goodland: Scripture
Union 1998

Chapter 21: Is it all right to use force on someone causing problems?
Children and crime, Bob Holman: Lion 1996

Chapter 22: Broken lives
Christianity and Child Sex Abuse, Hilary Cashman: SPCK 1993
Strong at the Broken Places, Linda Sandford: Virago Press 1991
The protector's handbook, Gerrilyn Smith: The Women's Press
Current government guidelines: *Working Together*, HMSO
1991, *The challenge of partnership in child protection – a prac-
tical guide*, HMSO 1995
PCCA Christian Childcare, PO Box 133, Swanley, Kent BR8
7UQ Tel: 01322 667207
NSPCC, 67 Saffron Hill, London EC1N 8RS Tel: 0171 242 1626
Kidscape, 152 Buckingham Palace Road, London SW1W 9TR
Tel: 0171 730 3300
Childline 0800 1111 (a number that should be shown in public
for the children to see)
Parentline – Contact 0268 757077 (a local number will be given
for parents)
London Rape Crisis Centre 0171 837 1600

Chapter 23: *I've got a school assembly: what do I do?*

Everyone can know (assemblies for multi-faith schools), CPAS

Assembly Point, Graham Knox and David Lawrence: Scripture Union 1990

A really great assembly, Grahame Knock and Chris Chesterton: Scripture Union 1992

Just think about that – 40 outlines for secondary assemblies, Phil Watson: Scripture Union

Schoolswork Handbook, Emlyn Williams: Scripture Union

Leading worship in schools, Janet King: Monarch 1990

The Best Time to Act, Paul Burbridge and Murray Watts: Hodder & Stoughton 1995

Scripture Union can be contacted at 207 Queensway, Bletchley, Milton Keynes, MK2 2EB

Youth for Christ: PO Box 5254, Halesowen, West Midlands Ba63 3DG

Chapter 24: *Am I really expected to encourage my youth group in street evangelism?*

Youth work and the mission of God, Pete Ward: SPCK 1997

Evangelism made slightly less difficult: how to interest people who aren't interested, Nick Pollard: InterVarsity Press 1997

Gospel Exploded Bob Mayo

Keeping your cool while sharing your faith, Greg Johnson & Susie Shellenberger: Tyndale 1993

Groups without Frontiers, Phil Moon, Penny Frank and Terry Clutterham: CPAS

How shall we reach them, Michael Green & Alister McGrath Nelson: Word

Chapter 25: *I can't be expected to practice everything I preach, can I?*

Worth doing well, Edited by Timothy Broadshaw: Methodist Publishing House

Chapter 26: *Am I supposed to be a spiritual Guru?*

Both chapters 25 and 26 are about developing your own spiritual walk with God. Books that may help you do this are:

Loving God, Charles Colson: Marshall Pickering1983
Celebration of Discipline, Richard Foster: Hodder & Stoughton 1980
Tough minds, tender hearts, Jonathan Lamb: IVP 1997
Classics from Watchman, Nee: Kingsway 1997
Knowing God, Jim Packer: Hodder & Stoughton 1973
Walking with God, Rob Warner: Hodder & Stoughton 1998
What's So Amazing about Grace?, Philip Yancey